Contents

PREFACE   - 1 -

THE NEW SOCIETY   I   - 2 -

FOOTNOTES: - 6 -

II   - 7 -

FOOTNOTES: - 9 -

III   - 10 -

IV   - 12 -

FOOTNOTES: - 16 -

V   - 17 -

FOOTNOTES: - 21 -

VI   - 23 -

FOOTNOTES: - 36 -

VII   - 37 -

FOOTNOTES: - 39 -

VIII   - 40 -

IX   - 45 -

FOOTNOTES: - 52 -

X   - 53 -

FOOTNOTES: - 57 -

XI   - 59 -

FOOTNOTES: - 62 -

XII   - 63 -

FOOTNOTES: - 70 -

XIII   - 71 -

FOOTNOTES: - 80 -

THE EUROPEAN LIBRARY   - 81 -

The New Society

Walther Rathenau

Alpha Editions

This edition published in 2022

ISBN: 9789356785397

Design and Setting By

Alpha Editions

www.alphaedis.com

Email - info@alphaedis.com

PREFACE

WALTHER RATHENAU, author of *Die neue Gesellschaft* and other studies of economic and social conditions in modern Germany, was born in 1867. His father, Emil Rathenau, was one of the most distinguished figures in the great era of German industrial development, and his son was brought up in the atmosphere of hard work, of enterprise, and of public affairs. After his school days at a *Gymnasium*, or classical school, he studied mathematics, physics and chemistry at the Universities of Berlin and of Strassburg, taking his degree at the age of twenty-two. Certain discoveries made by him in chemistry and electrolysis led to the establishment of independent manufacturing works, which he controlled with success, and eventually to his connexion with the world-famous A.E.G.—*Allgemeine Electrizitätsgesellschaft*—at the head of which he now stands. During the war he scored a very remarkable and exceptional success as controller of the organization for the supply of raw materials. He is thus not merely a scholar and thinker, but one who has lived and more than held his own in the thick of commercial and industrial life, and who knows by actual experience the subject-matter with which he deals.[vi]

The present study, with its wide outlook and its resolute determination to see facts as they are, should have much value for all students of latter-day politics and economics in Europe; for though Rathenau is mainly concerned with conditions in his own land the same conditions affect all countries to a greater or less degree, and he deals with general principles of human psychology and of economic law which prevail everywhere in the world. It is not too much to say that "The New Society" constitutes a landmark in the history of economic and social thought, and contains matter for discussion, for sifting, for experiment and for propaganda which should occupy serious thinkers and reformers for many a day to come. His suggestions and conclusions may not be all accepted, or all acceptable, but few will deny that they constitute a distinct advance in the effort to bring serious and disinterested thought to the solution of our social problems, and in this conviction we offer the present complete and authorized translation to English readers.

———————

THE NEW SOCIETY

I

Is there any sign or criterion by which we can tell that a human society has been completely socialized?

There is one and one only: it is when no one can have an income without working for it.

That is the sign of Socialism; but it is not the goal. In itself it is not decisive. If every one had enough to live on, it would not matter for what he received money or goods, or even whether he got them for nothing. And relics of the system of income which is not worked for will always remain—for instance, provision for old age.

The goal is not any kind of division of income or allotment of property. Nor is it equality, reduction of toil, or increase of the enjoyment of life. It is the abolition of the proletarian condition; abolition of the lifelong hereditary serfage, the nameless hereditary servitude, of one of the two peoples who are called by the same name; the annulment of the hereditary twofold stratification of society, the abolition of the scandalous enslavement of brother by brother, of that Western abuse which is the basis of our civilization as slavery was of the antique, and which vitiates all our deeds, all our creations, all our joys.

Nor is even this the final goal—no economy, no society can talk of a final goal—the only full and final object of all endeavour upon earth is the development of the human soul. A final goal, however, points out the direction, though not the path, of politics.

The political object which I have described as the abolition of the proletarian condition may, as I have shown in *Things that are to Come*, be closely approached by a suitable policy in regard to property and education; above all, by a limitation of the right of inheritance. Of socialization in the strict sense there is, for this purpose, no need. Yet a far-reaching policy of socialization—and I do not here refer to a mere mechanical nationalization of the means of production but to a radical economic and social resettlement—is necessary and urgent, because it awakens and trains responsibilities, and because it withdraws from the sluggish hands of the governing classes the determination of time and of method, and places it in the hands that have a better title, those of the whole commonalty, which, at present, stands helpless through sheer democracy. For only in the hands of a political people does democracy mean the rule of the people; in those of an untrained and unpolitical people it becomes merely an affair of debating societies and philistine chatter at the inn ordinary. The symbol of German bourgeois democracy is the tavern; thence enlightenment is spread and there judgments are formed; it is the meeting place of political associations, the forum of their orators, the polling-booth for elections.

But the sign that this far-reaching socialization has been actually carried out is the cessation of all income without work. I say the sign, but not the sole postulate; for we must postulate a complete and genuine democratization of the State and public economy, and a system of education equally accessible to all: only then can we say that the monopoly of class and culture has been smashed. But the cessation of the workless income will show the downfall of the last of class-monopolies, that of the Plutocracy.

It is not very easy to imagine what society will be like when these objects have been realised, at least if we are thinking not of a brief period like the present Russian régime, or a passing phase as in Hungary, but an enduring and stationary condition. A dictatorial oligarchy, like that of the Bolshevists, does not come into consideration here, and the well-meaning Utopias of social romances crumble to nothing. They rest, one and all, on the blissfully ignorant assumption of a state of popular well-being exaggerated tenfold beyond all possibility.

The knowledge of the sort of social condition towards which at present we Germans, and then Europe, and finally the other nations are tending in this vertical Migration of the Peoples, will not only decide for each of us his attitude towards the great social question, but our whole political position as well. It is quite in keeping with German traditions that in fixing our aims and forming our resolves we should be guided not by positive but by negative impulses—not by the effort to get something but to get away from it. To this effort, which is really a flight, we give the positive name of Socialism, without troubling ourselves in the least how things will look— not in the sense of popular watchwords but in actual fact—when we have got what we are seeking.

This is not merely a case of lack of imagination; it is that we Germans have, properly speaking, no understanding of political tendencies. We are more or less educated in business, in science, in thought, but in politics we are about on the same level as the East Slavonic peasantry. At best we know—and even that not always—what oppresses, vexes and tortures us; we know our grievances, and think we have conceived an aim when we simply turn them upside down. Such processes of thought as "the police are to blame, the war-conditions are to blame, the Prussians are to blame, the Jews are to blame, the English are to blame, the priests are to blame, the capitalists are to blame"—all these we quite understand. Just as with the Slavs, if our good-nature and two centuries of the love of order did not forbid it, our primitive political instincts would find expression in a pogrom in the shape of a peasant-war, of a religious war, of witch-trials, or Jew-baiting. Our blatant patriotism bore the plainest signs of such a temper; half nationalism, half aggression against some bugbear or other; never a proud calm, an earnest self-dedication, a struggle for a political ideal.

We have now a Republic in Germany: no one seriously desired it. We have at last established Parliamentarianism: no one wanted it. We have set up a kind of Socialism: no one believed in it. We used to say: "The people will live and die for their princes; our last drop of blood for the Hohenzollerns"—no one denied it. "The people mean to be ruled by their hereditary lords; they will go through fire for their officers; rather death than yield a foot of German soil to the foe." Was all this a delusion? By no means; it was sincere enough, only it did not go deep. It was the kind of sincerity which depends on not knowing enough of the alternative possibilities.

When the alternatives revealed themselves as possible and actual, then we all turned republican, even to the cottagers in Pomerania. When the military strike had broken down discipline, the officers were mishandled; when the war was lost, the fleet disgraced, and the homeland defiled, then we began to play and dance.

But was this frivolity? Not at all; it was a childish want of political imagination. The Poles, a people not remotely comparable to the German in depth of soul and the capacity for training talent, have for a century cherished no other thought than that of national unity, while we passively resign our territories. No Englishman or Japanese or American will ever understand us when we tell him that this military discipline of ours, this war-lust, did not represent a passion for dominion and aggression, but was merely the docility of a childish people which wants nothing, and can imagine nothing, but that things should go on as they happen, at the moment, to be.

We Germans know but little of the laws which govern the formation of national character. The capacity of a people for profundity is not profundity, either of the individual or of the community. It may express itself in the masses as mere plasticity and softness of spirit. The capacity for collective sagacity and strength of will demands from the individual merely a dry intelligence in human affairs, and egoism. It would be too much to say that our political weakness may be merely the expression of spiritual power, for the latter has not proved an obstacle to success in business. Indolence and belief in authority have their share in it.

But have we not been the classic land of social democracy, and have we not become that of Radicalism? Well, we have been, indeed, and are, with our submissiveness to authority and our capacity for discipline, the classic land of organized grumbling; and the classic land, too, of anti-semitism which deprived us of the very forces we stood most in need of—productive scepticism and the imagination for concrete things. Organized grumbling is not the same thing as political creation. A Socialism and Radicalism poorer in ideas than the post-Marxian German Socialism has never existed. Half of it was merely clerical work, and the other half was agitators' Utopianism of the cheapest variety.

Nothing was more significant than the fact that the mighty event of the German Revolution was not the result of affection but of disaffection. It is not we who liberated ourselves, it was the enemy; it was our destruction that set us free. On the day before we asked for the armistice, perhaps even on the day before the flight of the Kaiser, a plébiscite would have yielded an overwhelming majority for the monarchy and against Socialism. What I so often said before the war came true: "He who trains his children with the rod learns only through the rod."

And to-day, when everything is seething and fermenting—no thanks to Socialism for that—all intellectual work has to be done outside of the ranks of social-democracy, which stumbles along on its two crutches of "Socialization" and "Soviets." Orthodox Socialism is still a case of the "lesser evil," what the French call a *pis aller*. "Things are so bad that any change must be for the better." What is to make them better we are told in the socialist catechism; but *how* it is to do so, how and what anything is to become, this, the only question that matters, is regarded as irrelevant. It is answered by some halting and insincere stammer about "surplus value" which is to make everybody well off—and which would yield all round, as I have elsewhere shown, just twenty-five marks a head. Fifteen millions of grown men are pressing forward into a Promised Land revealed through the fog of political assemblies and in the thunder of parrot-phrases—a land from which no one will ever bring back a bunch of grapes.

If one would interrogate not the agitators, but their hearers, and find out what they instinctively conceive this land to look like, we should get the answer, timid and naïve but at the same time the deepest and shrewdest that it is possible to give—that it is a land where there are no longer any rich.

A most true and truthful reply! And yet a profound error silently lurks in it. You imagine, do you not, that in a land where there are no more rich people there will also be no more poor? "Why, of course not! How can there be poor people when there are no more rich?" And yet there will be. In the land where there are no more rich there will be *only* poor, only very poor, people.

Whoever does not know this and is a Socialist, that man is merely one of the herd or he is a dupe. He who knows it and conceals it is a deceiver. He who knows it, and in spite of that, nay, on account of that, is a Socialist, is a man of the future.

Though the crowd be satisfied with some dim feeling that this, anyhow, is the tendency of the times and that with this stream one must swim; though the more thoughtful contemplate the evils of the time and decide to put up with the *pis aller*; the responsible thinker is under the obligation of investigating the land into which the people are being led. We must know what it looks like, where there are no rich people and where no one can have an income without working for it, we must understand what we call the "new society" so as to be able to shape it aright.

FOOTNOTES:

Von Kommenden Dingen, by Walther Rathenau. Berlin. S. Fischer.

Workers' and Soldiers' Councils.

II

THE question is not very urgent.

As surely as the hundred years' course of the social World-Revolution cannot be arrested, so surely can we prophesy that the process cannot maintain all along the line the rapid movement of its beginning. The victorious and the defeated countries will have to work out to the end the changes and interchanges of their various phases, for in the historical developments which we witness to-day, we find mingled together the phenomena of organic growth and of disease; already we see that the Socialism of the healthy nations is different from that of the sick ones. It is in vain that those who are sick with the Bolshevist disease dream that they can infect the world.

The small daily and yearly movements in our realm of Central Europe cannot be determined beforehand, because they depend upon small, accidental, local, and external forces. The great and necessary issues of events can be predicted, but it would be folly to discuss their accidental flux and reflux. When an unguarded house is filled with explosives from the cellar to the roof, then we know that it will one day be blown up; but whether this will happen on a Sunday or a Monday, in the morning or in the evening, or whether the left door post will be left standing or no, it would be idle to inquire.

From the historical point of view it is of no consequence whether Radicalism may make an inroad here and there, or whether here and there the forces of reaction and restoration may collect themselves for a transitory triumph. The great movement of history, as we always find when a catastrophe has worked itself out, grows slower, and this retardation in itself looks like reaction. We, who are not accustomed to catastrophes, and who did not produce this first one, but rather suffered it, we, who easily get sea-sick after every rapid movement—think, for instance, of the former Reichstag—we shall certainly experience, as the first deep wave of the Revolution sinks into us, an aristocratic, dynastic, and plutocratic Romanticism, a yearning for the colour and glitter of the time of glory, a revolt against the spiritless, mechanical philanthrophy of unemployed orators of about fourth-form standard intellectually; against the monotonous and insincere tirades of paid agitators and their restless disciples; against laziness; ignorance, greed, and exaggeration masquerading as popular scientific economy; and against the brutal and extortionate upthrust from below. And so we shall arrive at the reverse kind of folly, an admiration and bad imitation of foreign pride and pomp, an arrogant individualism and a hardening of our human feeling. The intellectual war profiteers, who are all for radicalism to-day, will soon be wearing cornflowers in their button-holes.

For the third time we shall see an illustration of the naïve shamelessness of the turn-coat. The spiritual process of conversion is worth noticing; Paul was converted to be a converter. But the scurrying of the intellectual speculator from the position which has failed into the position which has won, with the full intention of scurrying back again if necessary, and always with the claim to instruct other people, is an expression of the alarming fact that life has become not an affair of inward conviction, but of getting the right tip.

The turn-coat movement began when a shortsighted crowd, incapable of judgment, and with their minds clouded with a few cheap phrases, expected from a quick and victorious war the strengthening of all the elements of Force, and feared to be left stranded. Even the most threadbare kind of liberalism appeared to be compromising, they clamoured for "shining armour." The most wretched victims in soul and body, who were obliged to flee forwards because they could not flee in any other direction, were called heroes, and the manliest word in our language, a word of which only the freest and the greatest are worthy, was degraded. One who has experienced the hate and fury of the turn-coats who poured contempt upon every word against the war and the "great days," is unable to understand how a whole people can throw its errors overboard without shame and sorrow—or he understands it only too well. At this day we are being mocked and preached at by the turn-coats of the second transformation, and to-morrow we shall be smiled at by those of the third.

But it does not matter. The moving forces of our epoch do not come from business offices nor from the street, the rostrum, the pulpit, or the professorial chair. The noisy rush of yesterday, to-day and to-morrow is only the furious motion of the outermost circle, the centre moves upon its way, quietly as the stars.

We have in our survey to leap over several periods of forward and backward movement and we shall earn the thanks of none of them. What is too conservative for one will be too revolutionary for another, and the æsthete will scornfully tell us that we have no fibre. When we show that what awaits us is no fools' paradise, but the danger of a temporary reverse of humanity and culture, then the facile Utopianist will shout us down with his two parrot-phrases, and when we, out of a sense of duty, of harmony with the course of the world and confidence in justice at the soul of things, tread the path of danger, precipitous though it be, then we shall be scorned by all the worshippers of Force and despisers of mankind.

But we for our part shall not pander either to the force-worshippers or to the masses. We serve no powers that be. Our love goes out to the People; but the People are not a crowd at a meeting, nor a sum-total of interests, nor are they the newspapers or debating-clubs. The People are the waking or sleeping, the leaking, frozen, choked, or gushing well of the German spirit. It is with that spirit, in the present and in the future, as it runs its course into the sea of humanity, that we have here to do.

FOOTNOTES:

The emblem of the Hohenzollerns.

The reference, apparently, is to the argument that any change must be for the better, and to the reliance on surplus value. See pp. 13, 14.

III

THE criterion which we have indicated for the socialized society of the future is a material one. But is the spiritual condition of an epoch to be determined by material arrangements? Is this not a confession of faith in materialism?

We are speaking of a criterion, not of a prime moving force. I have no desire, however, to avoid going into the material, or rather we should say mechanical, interpretation of history. I have done it more than once in my larger works, and for the sake of coherence I may repeat it in outline here.

The laws which determine individual destinies are reproduced in the history of collective movements. A man's career is not prescribed by his bodily form, his expression, or his environment; but there is in these things a certain connexion and parallelism, for the same laws which determine the course of his intellectual and spiritual life reflect themselves in bodily and practical shape. Every instant of our experience, all circumstances in which we find ourselves, every limb that we grow, every accident that happens to us, is an expression or product of our character. We are indeed subject to human limitations; we are not at liberty to live under water or in another planet; but within these wide boundaries each of us can shape his own life. To observe a man, his work, his fate, his body and expression, his connexions and his marriage, his belongings and his associations, is to know the man.

From this point of view all social, economic and political schemes become futile, for if man is so sovereign a being there is no need to look after him. But these schemes re-acquire a relative importance when we consider the average level of man's will-power, as we meet it in human experience—a power which, as a rule, shows itself unable to make head against a certain maximum of pressure from external circumstances. And again, these schemes are really a part of the expression of human will, for through them collective humanity battles with its surroundings, its contemporary world, and freely shapes its own destinies.

The inner laws of the community harmonize with those of the individuals who compose it. The fact that certain national traits of will and character are conditioned or even enforced by poverty or wealth, soil and climate, an inland or maritime position, tends to obscure the fact that these external conditions are not really laid on the people but have been willed by themselves. A people *wills* to have a nomadic life, or wills to have a sea-coast, or wills agriculture, or war; and has the power, if its will be strong enough, to obtain its desire, or failing that to break up and perish. It is the same will and character which decides for well-being and culture, or indolence and dependence, or labour and spiritual development. The Venetians did not have architecture and painting bestowed upon them because they happened to have become rich, nor the English sea-power because they happened to live on an island: no, the Venetians willed freedom, power and art, and the Anglo-Saxons willed the sea.

There is a grain of truth in the popular political belief that war embodies a judgment of God. At any rate character is judged by it; not indeed in the sense of popular politics, that one can "hold out" in a hopeless position, but because all the history that went before the war, the capacity or incapacity of politics and leadership is a question of character—and with us it was a question of indolence, of political apathy, of class-rule, philistinish conceit and greed of gain. Nowhere was this conception of the judgment of God so blasphemously exaggerated as with us Germans, when the lord of our armed hosts, at the demand of the barracks greedy for power, of the tavern-benches, the state-bureaus and the debating societies was summoned, and charged with the duty, forsooth, of chastising England— England, which they only knew out of newspaper reports! To-day this exaggeration is being paid for in humiliation, for God did not prove controllable, and His naïve blasphemers must silently and with grinding teeth admit that their foes are in the right when they, in their turn, appeal to the same judgment to justify, without limit, everything they desire to do.

After these brief observations on the psycho-physical complex, Spirit and Destiny, we hope we shall not be misunderstood when for the sake of brevity we speak as if the spirit of the new order were determined by its material construction, while in reality it incorporates itself therein. The structure is the easier to survey, and we therefore make it the starting-point of our discussion.

———————

IV

ALL civilisations known to us have sprung from peoples which were numerous, wealthy and divided into two social strata. They reached their climax at the moment when the two strata began to melt into one.

It is not enough, therefore, that a people should be numerous and wealthy; it must, with all its wealth and its power, contain a large proportion of poor and even oppressed and enslaved subjects. If it has not got these, it must master and make use of other foreign cultures as a substitute. That is what Rome did; it is what America is doing.

It is terrible, but comprehensible. For up to this point the unconscious processes of Nature, the law of mutual strife, has prevailed. So far, collective organizations have been beasts of prey; only now are they about to cross the boundaries of the human order.

Comprehensible and explicable. For all creations of culture hold together; one cannot pursue the cheaper varieties while renouncing the more costly. There is no cheap culture. In their totality they demand outlay, the most tremendous outlay known to history, the only outlay by which human toil is recompensed, over and above the supply of absolute necessaries.

The creations of civilisation, like all things living and dead, follow on each other—plants, men, beasts and utensils have their sequence generation after generation. Men must paint and look at pictures for ten thousand years before a new picture comes into existence. Our poetry and our research are the fruit of thousands of years. This is no disparagement to genius in work and thought, genius is at once new, ancient and eternal, even as the blossom is a new thing on the old stem, and belongs to an eternal type. When we hear that a native in Central Africa or New Zealand has produced an oil-painting we know that somehow or other he must have got to Paris. When a European artist writes or paints in Tahiti, what he produces is not a work of Tahitian culture. When civilisation has withered away on some sterilized soil, it can only be revived by new soil and foreign seed.

The continuity of culture, even in civilized times, can only, however, be maintained by constant outlay, just as in arid districts a luxuriant vegetation needs continuous irrigation. The flood of Oriental wealth had to pour itself into Italy in order to bring forth the bloom of Renaissance art. Thousands of patricians, hundreds of temporal and spiritual princes, had to found and to adorn temples and palaces, gardens, monuments, pageants, games and household goods in order that art and science, schooling, mastership, discipleship and tradition might grow up. The worship of foreign culture which characterized Germany in the seventeenth and half of the eighteenth centuries only meant that our soil was grown too poor to yield a crop of its own. The culture of the Middle Ages remained international only so long as the population of Europe was too sparse and the opportunities of work too scanty to occupy local energies; even in the thinly populated, Homeric middle-ages of Greece, the builder and the poet were not settled in one place, they were wandering artists. If to-day the Republic of Guatemala or Honduras should want a senate-house or a railway-station they will probably send to London or Paris for an architect.

Even technique in handicraft and industry, that typical art of civilization, cannot dispense with a great and continuous outlay on training, commissioning and marketing in order to maintain itself. Although it has not happened yet, there is no reason why a Serb or a Slovak should not make some important discovery if he has been trained at a European University and learnt the technical tradition. That will not, however, give rise to an independent and enduring Serbian or Slovakian technique, even though the costliest Universities and laboratories should be established in the country and foreign teachers called to teach in them. After all that, one must have a market in the country itself; expert purchasers, manufacturers, middle-men, a trained army of engineers, craftsmen, masters, workmen and a foreign market as well—in short, the technical atmosphere—in order to keep up the standard of manufacture and production.

A poor country cannot turn out products of high value for a rich one; it has not had the education arising from demand. In products relating to sport and to comfort, for instance, England was a model, but in France these products were ridiculously misunderstood and imitated with silly adornments, while on the other hand French products of luxury and art-industry were sought for by all countries. German wares were considered to be cheap and nasty, until the land grew rich, and brought about the co-operation of its forces of science and technique, production and marketing, auxiliary industries and remote profits, finance and commerce, education and training, judgment and criticism, habits of life and a sense of comparative values.

But human forces need the same nurture, the same outlay and the same high training, as institutions and material products. Delicate work demands sensitive hands and a sheltered way of life; discovery and invention demand leisure and freedom; taste demands training and tradition, scientific thinking and artistic conception demand an environment with an unbroken continuity of cultivation, thought and intelligence. A dying civilisation can live for a while on the existing humus of culture, on the existing atmosphere of thought, but to create anew these elements of life is beyond its powers.

Do not let us deceive ourselves, but look the facts in the face! All these excellent Canadians, with or without an academic degree, who innocently pride themselves on a proletarian absence of prejudice, are adoptive children of a plutocratic and aristocratic cultivation. It is all the same even if they lay aside their stiff collars and eye-glasses; their every word and argument, their forms of thought, their range of knowledge, their strongly emphasized intellectuality and taste for art and science, their whole handiwork and industry, are an inheritance from what they supposed they had cast off and a tribute to what they pretend to despise. Genuine radicalism is only to be respected when it understands the connexion of things and is not afraid of consequences. It must understand—and I shall make it clear—that its rapid advance will kill culture; and the proper conclusion is that it ought to despise culture, not to sponge on it. The early Christians abolished all the heathen rubbish and abominations, the early Radicals would have hurried, in the first instance, to pick out the plums.

Culture and civilization, as we see, demand a continuous and enormous outlay; an outlay in leisure, an outlay in working power, an outlay in wealth. They need patronage and a market, they need the school, they need models, tradition, comparison, judgment, intelligence, cultivation, disposition, the right kind of nursery—an atmosphere. One who stands outside it can serve it, often more powerfully with his virgin strength than one who is accustomed to it—but he must be carried along and animated by the breath of the same atmosphere. Culture and civilization require a rich soil.

But the richness of the soil is not sufficient; culture must be based upon, and increased by, contrast. Wealth must have at its disposal great numbers of men who are poor and dependent. How otherwise shall the outlay of culture be met? One man must have many at his disposal; but how can he, if they are all his equals? The outlay will be large, but it must be feasible; how can it, if the labour of thousands is not cheap? The few, the exalted, must develop power and splendour, they must offer types for imitation: how can they do that without a retinue, without spectators, without the herd? A land of well-being, that is to say, of equally distributed well-being, remains petty and provincial. When a State and its authorities, councils of solid and thrifty members of societies for this or that, take over the office of a Mæcenas or a Medici, with their proposals, their calculations, their objections, their control, then we get things that look like war-memorials, waiting-rooms, newspaper-kiosks and drinking-saloons. It was not always so? No; but even in the most penurious times it was kings who were the patrons.

But if culture is such a poison-flower, if it flourishes only in the swamp of poverty and under the sun of riches, it must and ought to be destroyed. Our sentiment will no longer endure the happiness and brilliance of the few growing out of the misery of the many; the days of the senses are over, and the day of conscience is beginning to dawn.

And now a timid and troubled puritanism makes itself heard: Is there no middle way? Will not half-measures suffice? No, it will not do; let this be said once for all as plainly as possible, you champions of the supply of "bare necessities" who talk about "daily bread" and want to butter it with the "noblest pleasures of art." It will not do!

No, half-measures will not do, nor quarter-measures. They might, if the whole world, the sick, the healthy and the bloated all together were of the same mind as ourselves. In Moscow it is said that people are expecting the world-revolution every hour, but the world declines to oblige. Therefore, if culture and civilization are to remain what they were, is there nothing for it but with one wrench to tear the poisoned garment from our body? Or—is there then an "or"? Let us see. We have a long way before us. First of all we must know how rich or how poor we and the world are going to be, on the day when there will be no income without working for it and no rich people any more.

If our economic system made us self-supporting we might arrange matters on the model of the Boer Republic which had all it needed, and now and then traded a load of ostrich feathers for coffee and hymn books. But we, alas! in order to find nourishment for twenty millions have to export blood and brains. And if, in order to buy phosphates, we offer cotton stockings and night-caps as the highest products of our artistic energies, and declare that they are all the soundest hand-work—for in our "daily bread" economy we shall have long forgotten how to work such devil's tools as the modern knitting-machine—then people will reply to us: in the first place we don't want night-caps, and if we did we can supply them for one-tenth of the cost; and our cotton goods will be sent back to us as unsaleable.

A world-trade, even of modest dimensions, can only be carried on upon the basis of high technical accomplishment, but this height of accomplishment cannot be attained on the basis of any penny-wise economy. Whoever wills the part must also will the whole, but to this whole belongs not merely the conception of a technique, but of a civilization, and indeed of a culture. One might as well demand of a music-hall orchestra which plays ragtime all the year round that once in the year, and once only, on Good Friday, it should pull itself together to give an adequate performance of the Passion Music of Bach.

FOOTNOTES:

By this figure the author seems to be referring to the population of the impoverished Germany of the future if the course of Socialism proceeds on wrong lines.

V

FOR some decades Germany will be one of the poorest of countries. How poor she will be does not depend on herself alone, but on the power and the will for mischief of others—who hate us.

However, poverty and wealth are relative terms; Germans are still richer on the average than their forefathers; richer than the Romans or Greeks. The standard of well-being is set by the best-off of the competitors, for he it is who determines the current standard of technique and industry, the methods of production, the minimum of labour and skill. We cannot, as we have already seen, keep aloof from world-competition, for Germany needs cheap goods. We must therefore try to keep step so far as we can.

Even if we shut our eyes and take no more account of our debt to foreign lands than we do of the war-tribute, we must admit that the average standard of well-being in America far surpasses the German. Goods are not so dear as with us, and the wages of the skilled worker amounts to between seven and ten dollars a day—more than 100 marks in our money; and many artisans drive to their workshops in their own automobiles.

If, now, we ask our Radicals how they envisage the problem of competition with such a country, which in one generation will be twenty-or thirty-fold as rich as we are, they will blurt out a few sentences in which we shall catch the word "Soviet system," "surplus value," "world revolution." But in truth the question will never occur to them—it is not ventilated at public meetings.

Among themselves they talk, albeit without much conviction, about "surplus value"—which has nothing whatever to do with the present question, and in regard to which it has been proved to them often enough that so far as it can be made use of at all, it only means about a pound of butter extra per head of the population.

The economic superiority of the Western powers, however, goes on growing, inasmuch as to all appearance they are getting to work seriously to establish the new economy (which we have buried) in the form of State Socialism. A healthy, or what is to-day the same thing, a victorious economy, does not leap over any of its stages; it will work gradually through the apparently longer, but constant, movement from Capitalism to State Socialism and thence to full Socialism; while we, it seems, want to take a shortcut, and to miss out the intervening stage. And we lose so much time and energy in restless fluctuations forward and backward, hither and thither, that this leap in advance may fall short.

If anything could be more stupid and calamitous than the war itself it was the time when it broke out. There was one thing which the big capitalism of the world was formed to supply, which it was able to supply, and, in fact, was supplying: the thing which not only justified capitalism, but showed it to be an absolutely necessary stage in the development of a denser population. This was the enrichment of the peoples, the rapid, and even anticipatory restoration of equilibrium between the growing population and the indispensable increase in the means of production; in other words, general well-being. The unbroken progress of America, and the almost unbroken progress of England will demonstrate that in one, or at most two, generations the power of work and the output of mechanism would have risen to such a pitch that we could have done anything we liked in the direction of lightening human labour and reconciling social antagonisms.

Alas, it was in vain! The rapid advance to prosperity of the people of Central Europe, who had been accustomed to thrift and economy, went to their heads; they fell victims to the poison of capitalism and of mechanism; they were unable, like America in its youthful strength, to make their new circumstances deepen their sense of responsibility; in their greedy desire to store as much as possible of the heavenly manna in their private barns they abandoned their destinies to a superannuated, outworn feudal class and to aspiring magnates of the bourgeoisie; they would not be taught by political catastrophes, and at last, in the catastrophe of the war, they lost at once their imaginary hopes, their traditional power and the economic basis of their existence.

Those who are now pursuing a policy of desperation are unconsciously building their hopes on the breakdown which brought them to the top: they are avowedly making the hoped-for revolution in the West the central point of their system. If the West holds out, they will be false prophets; but it will not only hold out, it will in the beginning at all events, witness a great and passionate uprising of imperialistic and capitalistic tendencies. If there is any one who did not understand that a policy based on hopes of other peoples' bankruptcy is the most flimsy and frivolous of all policies, he might well have learned it from the war.

Germany must forge her own destinies for herself, without side-glances at the good or ill fortune of others. Had time only been given us to pass naturally from the stage of a prolonged and corrupted childhood into that of a manly responsibility, our ultimate recovery would be assured. But we have to accomplish in months what ought to be the evolution of decades; our national training has left us without convictions, we have no eye for the true boundaries of rights, claims and responsibilities, and we hesitate as to how far we must or ought to go. Unprepared, weakened, impoverished and sick, we are required, at the most unlucky moment, to work out a new and unprecedented order of life. Before even the educated classes are capable of forming a judgment on the question, the most incapable masses of the rawest youth, of the lowest classes of society, are let loose, and sit upon the judgment-seat.

It is not only that we have been rich and have become very poor, but we were always politically immature, and are so still. If the order of Society is to be that of root-and-branch Socialism, it will mean the proletarian condition for all of us, and for a long time to come. There is no use in flattering ourselves and painting the future better than it is; the truth must be spoken with all plainness. If we work hard, and under capable guidance, each of us will at most have an effective income of 500 marks in pre-war values, or, say, 2000 marks for the family. This average will be higher if we proceed on the principles of the New Economy, but again will be reduced by the necessity for allowing extra pay for work of higher value. If to-day the average income available is markedly higher than the above, the reason is that we are living on our capital; we are living on the products of work which ought to be reserved for the maintenance and renewal of the means of production; in other words we are exhausting the soil and slaughtering our stock. We are also consuming what foreign countries give us on credit; in other words, we are living on borrowed money.

It is childish lying and deception to act on the tacit assumption that thoroughgoing Socialism means something like a garden-city idyll, with play-houses, open-air theatres, excursions, picturesque raiment and fire-side art. This in itself quite decent ideal of the average architect, art-craftsman and art-reformer if expressed in dry figures would, "at the lowest estimate" as they say, demand about fivefold the capacity for production attainable by the utmost exertions and with a ten hours' day *before the war*—before the downfall of our economy and our exploitation by the enemy.

To place one-third of our working-class in decent, freehold dwellings would alone, if the material and means of production sufficed, require the whole working-capacity of the country for two years. Even after the last manufacturer's villa-residence, the last palace-hotel, have long been turned into tenements, the solution of the most urgent part of the housing-question will still be an affair of decades. For the sake of the last remnant of our self-respect we must finally tear asunder that web of economic falsehood, woven out of ignorance, mental lethargy, concealment and illusion, which has taken the place of the political. Let us see any one attempt to prove that Germany can carry on, I do not say a well-off, but even a petty tradesman's kind of existence, unless our means of production can by some stroke of magic be multiplied tenfold—on paper it can be done with ease—or unless the production value (not turnover), which an adult working-man can with the utmost exertion bring into being in the course of a year does not many times exceed the average value of 2000 marks.

No doubt the young folk of our big cities promise themselves a merry time for six weeks when they have got power, the shops, the wardrobes and the wine-cellars into their hands. For the leaders, it may last a little longer than for the rank-and-file. And then, for those of the former who have any sense of honesty, will come a question of conscience, which may be delayed by printing paper-money, but cannot be solved by any appeal to the people.

If Bolshevism were the contrary to what it is—if it were a success, a thing not absolutely impossible in a peasant-State, we might understand the self-assurance of those who, in opposition to our forecast, expect everything from the will of the people, the Soviet system and the inspirations of the future. We do understand it in the case of the drawing-room communists, and the profiteer-extremists who are out not for the cause, but for power, and perhaps only for material objects.

I know that by these observations I am favouring the cause of those sorry dignitaries of a day, the Majority Socialists, but I cannot help that. The truth is not false because it favours one party, nor is falsehood truth because it harms the other. The Socialism now in power is doing the right thing, although it is doing it out of ignorance and helplessness—it is waiting, and getting steam up. It is better to do the right thing out of error than to do the wrong thing out of wisdom. Out of error: for besides omitting to do what ought not to be done it also omits the things it ought to do—among others, the introduction of the New Economy. It is like mankind before the Fall; it does not know good from evil, what is useful and what is noxious, what can be done and what cannot. Well—let it take its time; it shall have time enough.

This time must be turned to good account. When we have come to the end of these observations we shall understand what a huge task lies between us and the realization of the new social order. In this case the longest way round is the shortest way home. And even if Germany should choose the mountain road with its broad loops and windings, we shall stray often enough, and go backward now and then; while if, in impatient revolt, we try to climb straight up, we shall slip down lower than where we started. Let us never forget how mysteriously our social and political immaturity seems to be bound up with our once lofty and even now remarkable intellectuality and morality. We have not won our liberties, they have fallen into our laps; it was by the general breakdown, by a strike, by a flight, that Germany and her former rulers have parted company. These liberties, social and political, are not rooted in the soil, they can hardly be said to be prized among the treasures of life, it is not their ideal, but their material side which attracts us. Those who used to shout Hurrah! now cry "All power to the Soviets!" and the day will come when they will again shout Hurrah! Then we shall witness a real sundering of our different visions of the world, visions now buried under a mass of interests and speculations.

In any case, whether the change is to be catastrophic or evolutionary, the journey will be a long one, and every attempt to hurry it will only prolong it further; it will throw us back for years, or it may be decades. Above all things, we must know whither we are going. In order to adapt ourselves to a new form of society we must know what it *may* look like, what it *ought* to look like, and what it *will* look like. We shall find that Germany is not going to be landed in an earthly Paradise, but in a world of toil, and one which for a long period will be a world of poverty, of a penurious civilization and of a deeply-endangered culture. The unproved, parrot-phrases of a cheap Utopianism will grow dumb—those phrases which offer us entrance into the usual Garden of Eden with its square-cut, machine-made culture and gaudy, standardized enjoyments—phrases which assure us that when we have introduced the six-hours' working day and abolished private property, the cinema horrors will be replaced by classical concerts, the gin-shops by popular reading-rooms, the gaming-hells by edifying lectures, highway robberies by gymnastic exercises, detective novels by Gottfried Keller, bazaar-trifles and comic vulgarities by works of refined handicraft; and that out of boxing contests, racecourse betting, bomb exercises, and profiteering in butter, we shall see the rise of an era of humility and philanthropy.

In the Promised Land as we conceive it, the classes which are now the bearers of German culture will lose almost everything, while the gain of the proletariat will be scarcely visible. And yet for the sake of this scarcely visible gain we must tread the stony path that lies before us. Willingly and joyfully shall we tread it; for out of this, at first, dubious conquest of equal rights for all men will grow the might of justice, of human dignity, of human solidarity and unity.

That is truly work for a century, and yet for that very reason the hard path will lead to its reward. We must learn to know it, and to understand that it is a path of sacrifice. We must not accept the invitation of fools to a Christmas party—fools who will make the welkin ring with their outcries when they find out their self-deception. Let us tread our path of suffering with a pride which disdains to be consoled by illusions.

FOOTNOTES:

By surplus-value (*Mehrwert*) the author means all that is produced above and beyond the bare necessities of life.

Die Neue Wirtschaft, by Walther Rathenau (S. Fischer). In this brief study, Rathenau urges (1) the unification and standardization of the whole of German industry and commerce in one great Trust, working under a State charter, and armed with very extensive powers; and (2) a great intensification of the application of science and mechanism to production.

See p. 37, *note*.

Morality, *Sittlichkeit*, a word of broader meaning than "morality," for it comprehends not only matters of ethical right and wrong, but the general temper and habit of mind of a people as expressed in social life.

VI

IN order to throw some light into the obscurity of that social dreamland which no one seriously discusses because no one honestly believes in it, let us, as it were, cut out and examine a section from the fully socialized Germany of the future. Let us suppose that certain economic and social conditions have lasted for a generation or so, and have therefore become more or less stabilized. At a normal rate of progress this state of things should be reached about the end of this century.

To begin with, let us make two very optimistic assumptions—first, that technical progress in Germany shall have developed to a point at which we are no longer impossibly outclassed and distanced by foreign nations, and, secondly, that by a timely and far-reaching reform of education and culture (the lowest cost of which must be set down at about three milliards of marks) the complete breakdown of civilisation may be averted. This reform is one which must be taken in hand very early, for *after* the event its adoption is improbable. A third, less optimistic but on that account more probable assumption may be added to this—namely, that the Western countries shall have progressed towards Socialism more steadily and therefore more slowly, and that at the period of our comparison America shall find itself at the stage of State-Socialism, not of full socialization. We know that in making this assumption we are smoothing the way for attack to our professional opponents, uncritical and self-interested, who with one blast of the fanfare of world-revolution can scatter our further observations to the winds.

Full Socialism is characterized, as we have seen, by the abolition of all incomes that are not worked for, and the fact that there are no more rich. But this criterion must be limited in its application, for it can never be fully realized.

According to the theory and the laws every one must hold some appointment and be paid for his work, or for not working. What he is paid, however, he can at will utilize, or waste, or hoard up, or give, or gamble away, or destroy. He cannot invest it, or get interest on it or turn into capital, because these private undertakings or means of production will no longer exist.

Now each of these assumptions is so shaky that not only must trifling divergences and shortcomings be winked at, but the meshes of the system are so wide that only a rough approximation to the ideal is possible.

It is true that every one can be made to hold some appointment and be paid for some minimum of work, but no one can be prevented from devoting his leisure hours to some work of rare quality and turning it into value for his own purposes. He can make himself useful by subsidiary employment of an artistic, scientific or technical character, by rendering services or assistance of various kinds, by advising, or entertaining, or acting as a guide to strangers, or going on employment abroad, and no law can prevent him from turning his services into income even if he was merely paid in kind. Gaming and betting will flourish and many will grow rich by them. A man who has lost his money and who has exhausted his rights to an advance from the public institutions for that object will have recourse to lenders who will supply him with bread and meat and clothes, and who will make money by it. Similarly with people who are tempted to make acquisitions beyond their standard remuneration. On every side we shall see private stores of goods of all kinds, which will take the place of property as formerly understood.

There will be an enormous temptation to smuggling and profiteering which will reach a height far surpassing all scandals of the war and revolution periods. Foreigners and their agents, who look after the export trade "from Government to Government," will help hoarders and savers to turn their goods to account. Suppose citizens are attacked because their senseless expenditure is a mockery of their legal remuneration, they will say: I got this from friends—that I got by exchange—this came from abroad— my relatives in America sent me that. Law, control, terrorism, are effective just so long as there is not a blade of grass in the land—once remove the fear of hunger and they are useless. Great properties will arise, drawing interest both abroad and at home, and they will grow by evasions and bribery. The profiteer, the true child of the "great days," will not perish from the land, on the contrary, he will grow tougher the more he is persecuted, he will be the rich man of the future, and he will form a constant political danger if he and his fellows combine.

So long as we have not acquired an entirely new mentality, one which detaches men from possessions, which points them towards the Law, which binds the passions, and sharpens the conscience, so long will the principle of "No rich people and no workless income" have to be contracted into the formula, "There ought to be none."

Without this profound alteration of mentality, even the legally prescribed incomes will exhibit quite grotesque variations, and will adapt themselves to the rarity-value of special gifts, to indispensable qualities, to favouritism, with a crudity quite unknown to-day. A scarcity of Ministers, a Professor's nourishment, and soldiers' supplies, will then as now be met according to the law of supply and demand. Consider what ten years' practice in the war for wages and strike-management, with the public in it as partisans, will bring with it in the way of favouritisms, celebrities, and indispensabilities. Popular jockeys, successful surgeons, managers of sports' clubs, tenors, demimondaines, farce-writers and champion athletes could, even to-day, if they were class-conscious and joined together to exploit their opportunities, demand any income they liked. Even as a matter of practical political economy, the cinema-star (or whatever may succeed her) will be able to prescribe to the Government what amount of adornments, drawn from Nature or Art, are necessary for her calling, and what standard of life she must maintain in order to keep herself in the proper mood.

Organizers, popular leaders, authors and artists will announce and enforce their demands to the full limit of their rarity-value. At a considerable distance below these come the acquired and more or less transferable powers and talents. The Russians for the first few months believed in a three-fold order of allowances, rising within a limit of about one to two. If the ideas now prevailing have not undergone a radical change, then we may, in the society of the future, look for divergences of income in the limit of one to a thousand.

Therefore the principle that there shall be no more rich people must again be substantially limited. We must say, "There will be people receiving extraordinary incomes in kind to which must be added the claims to personal service which these favoured persons will lay down as conditions of their work."

In its external, arithmetical structure, the fabric of life and its requirements in the new order will resemble that of to-day far more closely than most of us imagine—on the other hand, the inward and personal constitution of man will be far more different. Already we can observe the direction of the movement.

Extravagance and luxury will continue to exist, and those who practise it will be, as they are to-day, and more than to-day, the profiteers, the lucky ones, and the adventurers. Excessive wealth will be more repulsive than it is now; whether it will be less valued depends upon the state of public ethics, a topic which we shall have to consider later. It is probable that in defiance of all legislation wealth will turn itself into expenditure and enjoyment more rapidly and more recklessly than to-day.

But the relics of middle-class well-being will by that time have been consumed; the families which for generations have visibly incorporated the German spirit will less than others contrive to secure special advantages by profiteering and evading the laws; as soon as their modest possessions are taxed away or consumed they will melt into the general mass of needy people who will form the economic average of the future.

The luxury which will exhibit itself in streets and houses will have a dubious air; every one will know that there is something wrong with it, people will spy and denounce, and find to their disgust that nothing can be proved; the well-off will be partly despised, partly envied; the question how to suppress evasions of the law will take up a good half of all public discussions, just as that of capitalism does now. The hateful sight of others' prosperity cannot, even at home, not to mention foreign countries, be withdrawn from the eyes of the needy masses; capitalism will have merely acquired another name and other representatives.

The fact that the average of more or less cultivated and responsible folk are plunged in poverty will not be accepted as the consequence of an unalterable natural law, nor as a case of personal misfortune; it will be set down to bad government, and the rising revolutionary forces of the fifth, sixth and seventh classes will nourish the prevailing discontent in favour of a new revolt. For the greater uniformity of the average way of life and its general neediness will not in itself abolish the division of classes. I have already often enough pointed out that no mechanical arrangements can avail us here.

At first there will be three, or more probably four classes who, in spite of poverty, will not dissolve in the masses, and who, through their coherence and their intellectual heritage are by no means without power. The Bolshevist plan of simply killing them out will not be possible in Germany, they are relatively too numerous; persecution will weld them closer together, and their traditional experiences, habits of mind, and capacity, will make it necessary to have recourse to them and employ them again and again.

The first of these classes is that of the feudal nobility. Their ancient names cannot be rooted out of the history of Germany, and even in their poverty the bearers of these names will be respected—all the more if, as we may certainly assume, they maintain the effects of their bodily discipline, and the visible tradition of certain forms of life and thought. They will be strengthened by their mutual association, their relationship with foreign nobility will give them important functions in diplomacy; these are two elements which they have in common with Catholicism and Judaism. They will retain their inclination and aptitude for the calling of arms and for administration; their reactionary sentiments will lead now to success, now to failure, and by both the inner coherence of the class will be fortified. Finally, the inevitable reversion to an appreciation of the romantic values of life will make a connexion with names of ancient lineage desirable to the leading classes, and especially to the aristocracy of officialism.

This aristocracy of officialism forms the second of the new strata which will come to light. The first office-bearers of the new era, be their achievements great or small, are not to be forgotten. Their descendants are respected as the bearers of well-known names; in their families the practice of politics, the knowledge of persons and connexions are perpetuated; fathers, in their lifetime, look after the interests of sons and daughters and launch them on the same path. From these, and from the first stratum, the representatives of Germany in foreign lands are chosen, and in this way a certain familiarity with international life and society will be maintained. They will have the provision necessary for their position abroad, and will also find ways and means to keep up a higher standard of life at home. Persons in possession of irregular means of well-being will offer a great deal to establish connexions with these circles, which control so many levers in the machine of State.

The third group consists of the descendants of what was once the leading class in culture and in economics. Here we find a spirit similar to that of the refugees, *émigrés* and Huguenots of the past. The lower they sink in external power, the more tenaciously they hold to their memories. Every family knows every other and cherishes the lustre of its name, a lustre augmented by legendary recollections, all the more when the achievements of their class are ostentatiously ignored in the new social order. People spare and save to the last extremity in order to preserve and hand down some heirloom—a musical instrument, a library, a manuscript, a picture or two. A puritanical thrift is exercised in order, as far as possible, to maintain education, culture and intellectuality on the old level; to this class culture, refinement of life as an end in itself, the practice of religion, classical music, and artistic feeling will fly for refuge. No other class understands this one; it holds itself aloof, it looks different from the rest in its occupations, its habits, its garb and its forms of life. It supplies the new order with its scholars, its clergy, its higher teaching power, its representatives of the most disinterested and intellectual callings. Like the monasteries of the Middle Ages, it forms an island of the past. Its influence rises and falls periodically, according to the current ideas of the time, but its position is assured by its voluntary sacrifices, by its knowledge and by the purity of its motives.

A fourth inexpugnable and influential stratum will in all probability be formed by the middle-class landowners and the substantial peasants. Even though the socialization of the land should be radically carried through— which is not likely to be the case—it will remain on paper. A class of what may be called State-tenants, estate-managers, or leaders of co-operative organizations will very much resemble a landowning class. Its traditional experience and the ties that bind it to the soil make it a closed and well-defined body, self-conscious and masterful through the importance of its calling, its indispensability and its individualism. It suffers no dictation as regards its manner of life. Here we shall see the conservative traditions of the country strongly mustered for defence, incapable of being eliminated as a political force, and forming a counterpoise to the radical democracy of the towns.

Everywhere we find a state of strain and of cleavage. The single-stratum condition of society cannot be reached without a profound inward change; politics are still stirred and shaken by conflicts, and society by the strife of classes. A very different picture from the promised Utopian Paradise of a common feeding-ground for lions and sheep!

We are all aggrieved by the illegal opulence of the profiteers, but we are all liable to the infection. The feudalistic Fronde awaits its opportunity. The aristocracy of office endeavours to monopolize the State-machine. The *émigrés* of culture find themselves looked askance at, on suspicion of intellectual arrogance, and they insist that the country cannot get on without them. The agriculturalists are feared, when they show a tendency to revolt against the towns. The ruling class, that is to say the more or less educated masses of the city-democracy, looks in impatient discontent for the state of general well-being which refuses to be realized, lays the blame alternately on the four powerful strata and on the profiteers, and fights now this group now that, for better conditions of living.

But the conditions of living do not improve—they get worse. The level of the nation's output has been sinking from the first day of the Revolution onwards. The absolute productivity of work, the relative efficacy and the quality of the product, have all deteriorated. With a smaller turnover we have witnessed a falling-off in the excellence of the goods, in research-work, and in finish. Industrial plant has been worked to death and has not yet recovered. Auxiliary industries, accessories and raw materials have fallen back. High-quality workmanship has suffered from defective schooling, youthful indiscipline and the loss of manual dexterity. The new social order has lost a generation of leaders in technique, scholarship and economics. Universities, with all institutions of research and education, have suffered from this blank. Technical leadership is gone, and the deterioration in quality has reacted detrimentally on output. We can now turn out nothing except what is cheap and easy, and what can be produced without traditional skill of hand, without serious calculation and research. For all innovations, all work of superior quality, Germany is dependent on the foreigner. The atmosphere of technique has vanished, and the stamp of cheap hireling labour is on the whole output of the country.

In the weeks of the Revolution street orators used to tell us that five hundred Russian professors had signed a statement that the level of culture had never been so high as under Bolshevism. And Berlin believed them! To educate Russia it would take, to begin with, a million elementary schools with a yearly budget of several dozen milliards of roubles, and a corresponding number of higher schools and universities: if every educated Russian for the next twenty years were to become a teacher, there would not be enough of them—not to speak of the requirements of transport, of raw materials and of agriculture. The fabric of a civilization and a culture cannot be annihilated at one blow, nor can it grow up save in decades and centuries. The maintenance of the structure demands unceasing toil and unbroken tradition; the breach that has been made in it in Germany can only be healed by the application in manifold forms of work, intellect and will; and this hope we cannot entertain.

But we have not yet done with the question of social strata and inward cleavage. Revolutionary threats are causing strife every day. Revolution against revolution—how is this possible? We are not speaking of a reactionary revolution but of the "activist."

In an earlier work I discussed the theory of continuous revolution. Behind every successful revolutionary movement there stands another, representing one negation more than its predecessor. Behind the revolt of the aristocracy stood that of the bourgeoisie, behind that of the bourgeoisie stood Socialism. Behind the now ruling fourth class rises the fifth, and a sixth is coming into sight. If a ninth should represent pure Anarchism, we may see an eleventh proclaiming a dictatorship, and a twelfth standing for absolute monarchy.

To-day the Majority Socialists are in power, that is to say the Right section of the fourth class. This is composed of the older, trained and work-willing Trade Unionists, who are amazed at the Revolution, who do not regard it as quite legitimate, but who are determined to defend the *status quo* in so far as a certain degree of self-determination and elbow-room in the material conditions of life still remain to them.

The Left section consists of youths and of persons disgusted with militarism, ignorant of affairs but cherishing a certain independence of judgment; still ready for work but equally so for politics. To these, as a "forward" party, the doctrinaire theorists have allied themselves. The designation of the party "The Independents" is characteristic; its goal, "All power to the Soviets," is a catchword from Russia.

A fifth class is now emerging—the work-shy. The others call them the tramp-proletariat, the disgruntled, the declassed, who set their hopes on disorder. Their goal is still undetermined—their favourite expression is "bloodhound," when those in power, or Government troops, are referred to.

Then comes the sixth class, still partly identified with the Left of the fourth and embryonically attached to the fifth. These are the indomitable loafers and shirkers, physically and mentally unsound, aliens in the social order, excluded by their sufferings, their punishments, their vices and passions; self-excluded, repudiators of law and morality, born of the cruelty of the city, pitiable beings, not so much cast out of society as cast up against it, as a living reproach to its mechanical organization. If these ever come into the light in politics, they will demand a kind of syndicalistic communism.

That is as far as we can see at present into the as yet unopened germs of continuous revolutionary movement. In these are contained the infinite series of all principles that can conceivably be supported; and it would be wholly false to see in this series merely so many successive steps in moral degeneration, even though the earlier stages should proceed on a flat denial of ethical principles. Later on will come revivals and restorations, political, ethical and religious, and each time we shall see the rising stratum attaching to itself strays and converts, above all, the disappointed and ambitious, from those that went before.

But the number of revolutions will grow till we lose count of them, and each, however strenuously it may profess its horror of bloodshed, will have only one hope and possibility: that of defending itself by armed force against its successor. The game is a grotesquely dishonest one, because every aspirant movement will cast against its forerunner the charge of ruling by bloodshed, while it itself is already preparing its armed forces for the conflict.

It is therefore wholly vain to hope that an advanced social organization implies stability, that a brotherhood mechanically decreed will exclude further revolutions, and will establish eternally an empire of righteousness and justice according to any preconceived pattern.

The fiercest hatred will prevail amongst those who are most closely associated—for instance, between handworkers and brainworkers, between leaders and followers; and this hate will be all the more inappeasable when it is open to every one to rise in the world, and none can cherish the excuse that he is the victim of a social system of overwhelming power. To-day this hatred is masked by the general class-hatred—hatred of the monopolists of culture, of position and of capital.

At the bottom of it, however, lies even to-day the more universal hatred of the defeated for the victor, and when those three monopolies have fallen, it will emerge in its original Cain-like form. It cannot be appeased by any mechanical device. Human inequality can never be abolished, human accomplishment and work will always vary, and the human passion for success will always assert itself.

We have discussed the material foundation and the stratification of the German people when full socialization has been realized. Let us now forecast the manner of their existence.

The future community is poor; the individual is poor. The average standard of well-being corresponds, at best, to what in peace-time one would expect from an income of 3000 marks. But the requirements of the population are not mediævally simplified—they could not be, in view of the density of the population and the complexity of industrial and professional vocations. They are manifold and diverse, and they are moreover intensified by the spectacle of extravagance offered by the profiteering class and the licence of social life. The traditional garden-city idyll of architects and art-craftsmen is a Utopia about as much like reality as the pastoral Arcadianism of Marie Antoinette.

All things of common use are standardized into typical forms. It must not be supposed, however, that they are based on pure designs and models. The taste of the artist will clash with that of the crowd, and since the former has no authority to back him he will have to compromise. The compromise, however, consists in cheap imitation of foreign models, for in foreign countries art-industry will exist, and no legislation can prevent its products from finding their way (in reproductions or actual examples) into Germany and being admired there. Our half or wholly imitative products are turned out as cheaply as possible, in substitute-materials, and are made as well or as ill as the relics of our craftsmanship permit, or as our existing machinery for the purpose is capable of. Cheapness and ease of manufacture are the principles aimed at, for even with narrow means no one will want to do without certain things; fashions still prevail, and will have to be satisfied with things that do not last, but can be constantly changed.

How far will a new system of education tend to simplify the needs of men and women and to purify their taste? Probably very little, for good models will be lacking, poverty is not fastidious, and the taste of the populace is the sovereign arbiter. But on this taste it depends whether vulgar ornaments and gewgaws, frivolities and bazaar-horrors, are to satisfy the desires of the soul.

Objects of earlier art and industry have been alienated through need of money or destroyed by negligence. Here and there one may find an old cup or an engraving, as we do to-day in plundered territories, but these things are disconnected specimens; all they can do is occasionally to interest an artist. Whoever wants to procure some object or to get something done which has not been standardized in the common range of approved requirements must gain it by a tedious course of pinching and saving. Personal possessions in the way of books, musical instruments, works of art, as well as travel outside the prescribed routes are rarities; a tree of one's own, a horse of one's own are legendary things.

Thus luxury in its better aspect has gone to ruin quicker than in the bad. All outlay devoted to culture, to beauty, to invigoration has dried up; all that survives is what stimulates, what depraves and befouls; frivolities, substitutes and swindles. What we have arrived at is not the four-square simplicity of the peasant-homestead, but a ramshackle city suburb. To some of us it is not easy, and to many it is not agreeable to picture to themselves the aspect of a thoroughly proletarianized country, and the difficulty lies in the fact that the popular mind has, as it were by universal agreement, resolved to conceive the future on a basis of domestic prosperity about tenfold as great as it can possibly be. The leaders and office-holders of the proletariat have an easy task in convincing themselves and others that what they approve and are struggling for is the so-called middle-class existence with all the refinement and claims of historic culture. Tacitly, as a matter of course, they accept what plutocracy has to give them, and imagine that the loans they take up from the civilization and culture of the past can be redeemed from the social gains of the future.

The stages at which a nation arrives year by year, can be estimated by its building. In the new order, little is being built. Apart from certain perfunctory garden-cities, which are being erected for the principle of the thing, to meet the needs of a few thousand favoured households, and which perhaps will never be finished, we will for decades have to content ourselves with new subdivisions and exploitation of the old buildings; old palaces packed to the roof with families, will stand in the midst of vegetable gardens and will alternate with empty warehouses in the midst of decayed cities. In the streets of the suburbs the avenues of trees will be felled, and in the cities grass will grow through the cracks of the pavement.

For a long time it used to be believed that the passion of the landscape painters of the seventeenth century for introducing ruins with hovels nestling among them arose from a feeling for romance. This is not so—they only painted what they saw around them after the ravages of the Thirty Years' War. It must not be supposed, however, that the forecast in these pages is based on the consequences of the war; these no doubt must darken our picture of the future; but the shadows, which I have put in as sparingly as I could, are essentially the expression of a greatly reduced economic efficiency, combined with the uniformity produced by the general proletarianization of life with the absence of any correcting factor in individual effort of a rational character and of the influence of higher types.

A brighter trait in the material conditions of life will be formed by effort of a collective character, such as even the most penurious community may be able to undertake. The more severely the domestic household has to pinch, and the more unattractive it thereby becomes, the more completely will life be forced into publicity. Private claims and aspirations, which cannot be satisfied, will be turned over to the public. Men will gather in the streets and places of public resort, and have more mutual intercourse than before, since every transaction of life, even the most insignificant, will have to be a subject of discussion, agreement and understanding. In all the arrangements of social life, *e.g.* for news, communications, supplies, discussion and entertainment, and demands will be made and complied with for greater convenience and comprehensiveness, for popular æsthetics and popular representation. In these arrangements and in these alone Art will have to find its functions and its home. Public buildings, gardens, sanatoriums, means of transit and exhibitions will be established at great cost. All the demands of the spirit and of the senses will seek their satisfaction in public. There will be no lack of popular performances, excursions, tours and conducted visits to collections; of clubs, libraries, athletic meetings and displays. The aspect of this tendency from the point of view of culture and ethics we have still to consider; in its social aspect (apart from the fact that it causes a vacuum in the home and forces young people to the surface of life, and in spite of its mechanical effect) it will act as a comforting reminiscence of the civic commonalty and solidarity of mediæval times.

In considering the spiritual and cultural life of a fully socialized society, we have to start with the assumption that any one man's opinion and decision are as good as another's. Authority, even in matters of the highest intellectual or spiritual character, only exists in so far as it is established, acknowledged and confirmed either by direct action of the people's will, or indirectly through their representatives. Every one's education and way of life are much the same; there are no secrecies, no vague authority attaching to special vocations; no one permits himself to feel impressed by any person or thing. Every one votes, whether it be for an office, a memorial, a law, or a drama, or does it through delegates or the delegates of delegates. Every one is determined to know the how and where and why of everything—just as to-day in America—and demands a plausible reason for it. The reply, "This is a matter you don't understand," is impossible.

Everything is referred to one's own conscience, one's own intelligence, one's own taste, and no one admits any innate or acquired superiority in others. In debate, the boundaries between the ideal and the practicable are obliterated; for on the one hand every one is too much preoccupied with material needs, and on the other, too confident, too unaccustomed to submit himself to what in former days was called a deeper insight, too loosely brought up to let himself be taught. We never, therefore, hear such judgments as: This, although it is difficult, is a book to be read; this drama ought to have been produced although it is not sensational; I don't myself care for this memorial, but it must remain because a great artist made it; this is a necessary branch of study, although it has no practical application; I will vote for this man on account of his character and ability, although he has made no election-promises. On the other hand, the following kind of argument will have weight: This historic building must be demolished, for it interferes with traffic; this collection must be sold, for we need money; we need no chair of philosophy, but we do need one for cinema-technique; these ornamental grounds are the very place for a merry-go-round; tragedies are depressing, they must not be performed in the State theatres. Let us recall certain oversea legislation—carried out, be it noted in countries still swayed by the traditional influence of culture—and these examples will not seem exaggerated.

Where there is no appeal to authority, where none need fear disapproval or ridicule, where convenience is prized and thrift rules supreme, there thought and decision will be short-breathed, and will never look beyond the needs of the day. Who will then care for far-off deductions, for wide arcs of thought? Calculation comes to the front, everything unpractical is despised; opinions are formed by discussion, everyday reading and propaganda. Men demand proofs, success, visible returns. The fewer the aims, the stronger will be their attraction. People are tolerant, for they are used to hearing the most varied opinions, and all opinions have followers, from the water-cure to Tâoism; but the only opinion of any influence is that whose followers are many.

Public opinion settles everything. The champions of absolute values have to accommodate themselves to the law of competition. Religious teaching has to seek the favour of the times by the same methods as a new system of physical culture. A work of art must compete for votes. Only by popularity-hunting can anything come to life; there will be no doing without much talking. As in the later days of Greece, rhetoric and dialectic are the most powerful of the arts.

And since manual labour cherishes silently or openly a bitter grudge against intellectual labour, the latter has to protect itself by a pretence of sturdy simplicity; when two teachers are competing for the head-mastership of a classical school each tries to prove that he has the hornier hand.

Most things in this new order are decided by weight of numbers. Advertisement and propaganda are banished from socialized industry and commerce; instead, they compete in the service of personal and ideal aims—in elections, theatres, systems of medicine, superstitions, arts, appointments, professorships, churches.

Art has for the third time changed its master—after the princes, Mæcenas, the middle-class market; after Mæcenas, the plebs, and export trade. Whether by means of representation through gilds, by compulsion, by patronage, or by favour, Art has become dependent; it must explain, exhort, contend; it can no longer rest proudly on itself. It must aim at getting a majority on its side, and this it can only do by sensationalism. Like all other features of intellectual life, it must march with the times. Like all technique, research, learning and handicraft it suffers through the loss, for several generations, of tradition and hereditary skill, but together with this drop there is also a drop in the character of the demand; quality has given way to actuality.

Certain reactions based on practical experience are not excluded; the constant comparison with the past and with foreign countries will show the value of the cultivation of a science, of an art which has no fixed prepossessions and serves no immediate aims. Measures are taken, though without much conviction, by free Academies or the like, to win back something of this; but the atmosphere is not favourable to such attempts, and an artificial and sterile discipline is all that can result.

The general tone is that of an excitable, loquacious generation, bent on actualities and matters of practical calculation, fonder of debate than of work, not impressed by any authority, prizing success, watching all that goes on abroad, taking refuge in public from the sordidness of private life, and passionately hostile to all superiority. Through the constant secession of elements to which this tone is antipathetic a kind of natural selection is constantly taking place, and the political defencelessness of the transition period favours disintegrating tendencies of foreign origin. The carving away of ancient German territories works in the same direction. Apart from the varying influence of the four strata already referred to, the general tone will be set by the half-Slavonic lower classes of Middle and North Germany, who have brought about and who control the existing conditions, and by the other elements which have been assimilated to these.

In place of German culture and German intellectuality we have a state of things of which a foretaste already exists in parts of America and of Eastern Europe. The fully socialized order, repelling all tutelage through those strata which possess a special tradition, outlook and mentality, has created its own form of civilization.

FOOTNOTES:

Rathenau means that it cannot be entertained except on the hypothesis of the profound *inward* change, which is to be discussed later on.

Kritik der dreifachen Revolution. S. Fischer.

The classes referred to are (1) the old aristocracy, (2) the aristocracy of officialism, (3) that of traditional middle-class culture; (4) the mass of what is called Socialism.

£150 in pre-war values. By thrift, by co-operation, and by the cheapness of the public services generally, a surprisingly high standard of life could be maintained on this kind of income in pre-war Germany.

Aktualität; as, for instance, reference to current topics.

VII

THOUGHTFUL and competent judges to whom I have submitted the foregoing section of my work have said to me: This is Hell. That is perhaps going too far, since those who will live in that generation and who have themselves helped it into being will have become more or less adapted to their circumstances.

A large part of the proletariat of to-day will certainly not be daunted by the prospect, but will regard it as a distinct improvement on their present situation. That is the terrible fact, a fact for which we are responsible and for which we must atone, with what ruin to German culture remains to be seen.

Who, in this Age of Mechanism, who on the side of the bourgeoisie, who of our statesmen, our professors, our captains of industry, above all who of our clergy, has pitied the lot of the working-man? The statesmen, for peace' sake, worked out the Insurance Laws; the professors, with their emphatic dislike to the world of finance and their unemphasized devotion to the monopoly of their own stipends, preached a doctrinaire socialism; the clergy lauded the divinely-appointed principle of subordination; the great industrialists, wallowing in their own greed for power, money, favour, titles and connexions, scolded the workers for wanting anything. The silent subjugation of our brothers was assured through the laws of inheritance, our leaders put the socialistic legislation in fetters, freedom of combination was thwarted, electoral reform in Prussia was scornfully denied, demands for better conditions of living, conditions which to-day we think ridiculously low, were suppressed by force. And all the time, the cost of a single year of war, a tiny fraction of the war-reparations, would have sufficed to banish want for ever from the land. At last the millions of the defenceless and disappointed were driven into that war of the dynasties and the bourgeois, which was unloosed by the folly of years, the dazzlement of weeks, the helplessness of hours.

If the state of things I have foreseen is hell, then we have earned hell. And it ill becomes us to wrap ourselves in the superiority of our culture, to rebuke the masses for their want of intellect, their want of character, their greed, and to keep insisting on the unchangeability of human character, on the virtues of rulership and leadership, on the spiritual unselfishness and intellectual priesthood of the classes born to freedom. Where was this heaven-nurtured priestly virtue sleeping when Wrong straddled the land and the great crime was wrought? It was composing feeble anthologies and pompous theories, cooking its culture-soup, confusing, with true professorial want of instinct, 1913 with 1813—and putting itself at the disposition of the Press Bureau. *That* was the hour in which to fight for the supremacy of the spirit. Now romance comes, as it always does, too late.

What is romance in history? It is sterility. It is incapacity to imagine, still less to shape, the yet unknown. It is an inordinate capacity for flinging oneself with feminine adaptability into anything that is historically presented and accomplished—from Michael Angelo to working samplers. Fearing the ugly present and the anxious future, the romantic takes refuge with the dear good dead people, and spins out further what it has learned from them. But every big man was a shaper of his own time, a respecter of antiquity and conscious of his inheritance as a grown and capable man may be; not a youth in sheltered tutelage, but a master of the living world, and a herald of the future. "Modernity" is foolish, but antiquarianism is rubbish; life in its vigour is neither new nor antique, but young.

True it is indeed that we love the old, many-coloured, concrete, pre-mechanistic world; we cannot take an antique thing in our hands or read an antique word without feeling its enchantment. It is a joy to the heart, and one prohibited to no man, to dream at times romantic dreams, to live in the past, and to forget, as we do it, that this very dreaming, this very life, owes its charm to the fact that we are of another age. It is a magic like that of childhood—but to want to go back to it is not only childish, but a deliberate fraud and self-deception. We should realize, as I have shown years ago, that the difference of our age from that age is the ever-present fact of the density of our population. Any one who wants to go back, really wants that forty million Germans should die, while he survives. It is ignorant, it is insincere, to put on a frown of offended virtue and to say: For shame, what are you thronging into the towns for? Go back to the land; plough, spin, weave, ply the blacksmith's hammer, as did our forefathers, who were the proper sort of people. And leave the people like us, who think and write poetry and brood and dream for you, a house embowered in vines—there will be room enough for that!—Ah, you thinkers and brooders, what would you say if men answered you: No! Go yourself and spin in a factory, for you have shown clearly enough that your thinking and brooding are futile. All your fine phrases amount to nothing but the one dread monosyllable—Die! Are you so wicked as that, and know it? or so stupid, and know it not?

Thought is the most responsible of all functions. He who thinks for others must look after them, and if they live he may not slay them. It is therefore a mischievous piece of romantic folly to point us to the past. We must all pass through the dark gateway, and the sage has no right to growl: Leave me out—I am the salt of the earth! The first thing we have to do is to save humanity; not a selected pair in the Ark but the whole race, criminals and harlots, fools, beggars and cripples. We ourselves have cast down Authority, and there will be a crush, and many things will look very different from what the sages would wish and what the romantics dream. And if it is going to be hell for people like you and me, we must only accept it in the name of justice, and think of Dante's terrible inscription: "I was made by the Might of God, by the supreme Wisdom and by the primal Love."

But is it hell? That depends on ourselves.

FOOTNOTES:

In 1913 all Germany was celebrating with great pomp and warlike display the centenary of the liberation of the country from Napoleon, and also paying a huge property tax for the coming war.

> *Fecemi la divina Potestate*
> *La somma Sapienza e il primo Amore.*

This is part of the inscription over the gates of Hell in the *Inferno*, Canto III.

VIII

OUR description of the future order of society was tacitly based on the assumption that our mentality, our ethics, our spiritual outlook, would remain as they are at present.

This assumption is a probable one, but it is not irrevocably certain. What we have endeavoured to demonstrate is simply the obvious fact—the fact which our once so rigid but, since November, 1918, uprooted and flaccid intellectualism has forgotten—that our salvation is not to be found in any kind of mechanical apparatus or institutions. Institutions do not mean evolution. If institutions run too far ahead of evolution there will be reaction. When evolution runs too far, there is revolution.

At this point both groups of our opponents will start up against us.

The Radicals cry: Ha! only give us food, give "all power to the Soviets," let us have free-thought lectures, and mentality, insight, experience and culture will come of themselves.

The Reactionaries smile: Ho! this man has never learned that there is no such thing as evolution; that human character never changes.

I shall not answer either of these. They know, both of them, that they are saying what is not true.

Something of unprecedented greatness can and must take place; something that in the life of a people corresponds to the awakening of manhood in the individual.

In every conscious existence there comes a moment when the living being is no longer determined but begins to determine himself; when he takes over responsibility from the surrounding Powers, in order to shoulder it for himself; when he no longer accepts the forces that guide him, but creates them; when he no longer receives but freely chooses the values, ideals, aims and authorities whose validity he will admit; when he begets out of his own being the relations with the divine which he means to serve. For the German people this moment, this opportunity, has now arrived—or is for ever lost.

We have made a clear sweep of all authorities. The inherited influences which we accepted unconsciously have dropped away from us—persons, classes, dogmas. The persons are done with for the present. The classes, even though they may still keep up the struggle, are broken to pieces together with all the best that they contained: mentality, sense of honour, devotion, training, tradition. We can never reanimate them and never supply their place. Ideas and dogmas have long ago lost their cogency; the power they wielded through police and school, the power which we tried to prop up by a blasphemous degradation of religion and by developing the church as a kind of factory, is gone, and it would be a piece of mechanical presumption to suppose that we can breed them again for the sake of the objects they fulfilled. If we live and thrive, ideas and faiths will grow up of themselves.

We must of our own free choice lay upon ourselves a certain life-potency or faculty which we shall freely obey, and which shall be so broad and so buoyant that thought and creation can grow out of it. A deed without precedent only in its voluntary, conscious self-determination: for other peoples in earlier days also accepted these faculties, not indeed out of conscious choice, but from the hands of prophets, rulers and classes. Thus theocracy was laid upon Israel; the caste-system on the Indians; the idea of the city on the Greeks; empire on the Romans; the Church on the Middle Ages; commerce, plutocracy, colonial dominion, on the modern world; militarism on Germany. For these imposed forces men lived and died; they had only a mythical conception of where they came from, and they believed and some still believe them to be everlasting.

A thunder-stroke of destiny has at once stripped us bare and has opened our eyes. The tremendous choice is before us. Are we to reject it, and, blinded anew, to resign ourselves to the casual and mechanical laws of action and reaction, of needs and interests, and the competition of forces? Are we to recover ourselves, and enter into the intellectual arena of the nations, to begin a new and enduring life with no other guiding thought than that of self-preservation and the division of property? In the harbour of the nations is our ship to drift aimlessly while every other knows its course, whether to a near or distant port? Is that penurious Paradise which we have described, the goal of Germany's hopes and struggles?

Compared with us, the French movement of the eighteenth century had an easy task. All it had to do was to deny and demolish. When it had cleared away the wreckage of feudalism, at once a strong new class, the bourgeoisie, sprang up from the soil, more vigorous than its aristocratic forerunner, and it was able to take care of itself. And the bourgeoisie was also a class of defined boundaries, and already trained for its task; it had long ago taken over French culture, it alone had for a century been the champion of French ideas, it had acquired enthusiasm for the nation, for freedom, for militarism and for money; the aspirations for equality and fraternity were not indeed fulfilled, but the first mechanized and plutocratic state of the Continent came into being.

Germany, as we have seen, is not in the same position. When we are stripped we find no new stratum of culture growing up below the surface; society is simply dissolved, and in its place we find the masses, of which the most hopeful thing we can say is that they are an ordered body. Tradition has been torn in two. No—we have to build from the foundations up. But whether we shall build according to the changing needs of the seasons, according to the casual balance of forces, or according to an idea and a symbol—that is the question!

Our current Socialism has no qualms about bringing new nations to birth with the aid of a few simple apparatus and radical eliminations; it believes that the right spirit will soon enter in if only institutions are provided for it. It would be too severe to describe this way of thinking solely as contempt for or want of understanding of a spiritual mission. Socialism in its prevailing form arises indeed simply from material or so-called "scientific" conceptions (as if there could be a science of ideal aims and values): but it has, though only as a secondary object, annexed to itself the values of a spiritual faith—the latter are, as the language of the market has it, "thrown in." We have seen to what the material domination of institutions and apparatus is leading us. To national dignity, or to any mission for humanity, it does not lead.

What is unprecedented in our problem is not, as we have said, that a people should beget out of itself its own idea and mission. From the Jewish theocracy to the French rationalism, from the Chinese ancestor-worship to the pioneer-freedom of America, all the cultured peoples have brought this creative act to pass, although in formative epochs leading classes and leading men have born the responsibility and made it easy for their countrymen to become aware of their own unconscious spirit, and through this awareness and consciousness to isolate and intensify it.

What is unprecedented is just this: that the process should take place as a deliberate act of will, in democratic freedom, without pressure and compulsion of authority, in the consciousness of its necessity, on our own responsibility. Germany is not at present growing leaders and prophets, we are not in a formative stage, all authority has been scattered to the winds. It is true that we have one stratum of society which is capable of understanding the meaning of the task, but it is deeply cloven, the hatreds and interests of its parties make them more each other's enemies than the people's.

And yet it is this very class—not as possessor of means but as possessor of the tradition, which is capable, which is indispensable, and which is summoned to take in hand the transformation of the German spirit, to free it from the bonds of mechanism, of capitalism, of militarism, and to lead it to its true destinies. It cannot do this for itself alone, amid the blind bitterness of the war of classes; it cannot do it as a sovran leader relying on its deeper insight, for its and every other prestige has gone by the board; it can only do it by the way of service and sacrifice—it can only do it if the service and the sacrifice are approved and accepted.

The masses will not understand this sacrifice of service; but the more responsible of their leaders will. Not to-day, indeed, nor to-morrow; but on the day when experience has shown them that I am telling the truth. At first they will do as in Russia; when want becomes acute, they will seek to buy experience and tradition at a high price from individuals. But mentality and spirit cannot be bought—only labour and dexterity. Then gradually men will come to understand that the highest things are not marketable commodities, they are only given away. And at last the responsible leaders, those who rule in order to serve, will separate themselves from those of the Cataline type, who serve in order to rule.

So long has the narrow, parsonical, cynical contempt for the understanding of the lower classes prevailed—through our fault—a reversal to blind worship of the masses, of the immature and the unsuccessful, is not inexcusable. We are here to love mankind—all mankind, the outcast as well as the weak—every man and all men. But the masses are not quite the same thing as mankind. The masses who congregate in the streets and at public meetings are not communities consisting of whole men, but assemblages in which each man takes a part and is present, indeed, with his whole body, but by no means with his whole being. The masses are absent-minded; and presence of mind only comes to them when through the lips of some true prophet the Spirit descends upon them. But when that happens, they take no decisions; they do not get beside themselves; rather, they sink into themselves. Before the distortions of a mob orator, with his extravagant promises, the masses become merely a driven crowd eager for gain, not human souls. They are the concave reflector of passions and greeds that rage in the focal point of the speaker's rostrum; they return in concentrated form the rays that dazzle them. He who puts the masses in the judgment-seat, who looks for counsel and decision at their hands, has neither reverence nor love for man. Sooner or later the truth of this will be realized by all honourable men among their leaders.

The day is also far when the upper classes will come to their senses. They have never understood what the world is, nor what Germany is, nor what has happened to themselves. They see houses and fields, streets and trees very much as they were; they think, if they only play the game a little craftily at the beginning, everything will remain as it used to be, and they will come out all right in the end. It is just as when some merchant goes bankrupt for a million; for the first fortnight the servants wait at table as usual and the family eat off silver plate; the ruin is still on paper. But in a year's time everything is dispersed to the winds, and men have changed along with their utensils. When one sees for what trivialities people are fighting to-day one begins to understand how callously and shamelessly they gave up a thousand times over that which they had sworn to defend with the last drop of their blood; then none of them know what has really happened. In a few years' time they will know; and then they will fight no more for things that no longer exist; they will be meditating a general sacrifice to save what can still be saved, and what is worth saving.

———————

IX

GERMANY is a land without power, without poise, with its prosperity shattered, its authorities and its external aims annihilated, its intellect and its ethics at a low ebb. In such a condition, if we wish to understand the only kind of life-faculty which can save us from intellectual and spiritual death, give us force and inspiration to shape for ourselves and for the world the new social order of freedom, spirituality and justice, and in the true sense to "save" us, we must look ourselves and the German character in the face— this unknown, problematic character, which for a century in contradiction to its own inmost being, has been flattering and lulling itself with hackneyed and complacent phrases and unproved judgments. For we can undertake nothing and claim nothing which has not its prototype in our own soul and is not founded in our own past, our own traditions.

There is no people, not even the French, which in recent decades has administered to itself and digested so much praise as we have. We never discussed ourselves but at once the stereotyped toasts began. The more German culture declined, the more disgusting became our babble about it.

The persons through whose mouths we let ourselves be lauded were school-teachers without comparative knowledge, professional banquet-orators, nationalists who praised in the service of some interested hatred, and scholars with appointments who were simply commissioned to demonstrate that the Hohenzollern system was the last word of creation. No one dreamed of distinguishing this glorification of the German people from the apotheosis of the dynasties—to which we had vowed our heart's blood—and the profound insincerity of these declamations was shown by the indifference with which the dynasties, the main feature in the programme, were afterwards got rid of, and the affair of the heart's blood shelved.

We know the stereotyped phrases. German faith, French knavery. The world is to find healing in the German soul. We are the heroes—the others are hucksters. To be German means to do a thing for its own sake. We are a "race of thinkers and poets." We have Culture, the others merely Civilization. We alone are free—the others are merely undisciplined (or, as the case may be, enslaved). All this we owe to the favour of God and our education under the (here fill in Prussian, Bavarian or Saxon) reigning House, which all the world envies us. Clearly therefore we are destined for world-dominion; we have only to fall-to.

In one of these phrases, about doing things for their own sake, there is truth. All the more was it for us in particular a vice and a sign of degradation to let ourselves be dazzled by the shadowless transparency-picture of glorification that was offered to us. There were interests concealed in the game, and much lack of moral fibre, all of which we passed over in silence; it was out of place in our festal oratory.

It would be an equal or even a greater vice, only reversed, if we were now to despair of ourselves. Moderation was what we needed then; what we need now is vigorous and conscious self-possession. To-day it is no easy and attractive business to bring our strong qualities to the surface; it implies an amount of conviction which it is hard to attain, and self-depreciation means a pitiful faint-heartedness. But all sham goods offered by babblers, by selfish interests, prophets of hate and commercial travellers must go overboard.

We have never been a "race of thinkers and poets," any more than the Jews were a race of prophets, the French and Dutch a race of painters, or Königsberg a city of Pure Reason. The old German upper classes have, in three well-defined epochs, had force enough to throw up individuals of mighty endowments for music, poetry and philosophy; the former lower-classes, whose blood runs in nine-tenths of our present population, have scarcely contributed anything to these glories. They have in recent years shown themselves thoroughly industrious, plastic, apt for discipline, order-loving, intelligent, practical, honourable, trustworthy, warm-hearted, prudent and helpful, and adapted beyond all expectation to the mechanization of life and industry; of their power to produce talent we know little, except perhaps in the domain of research and technique, which are less a test of creative energy than of applied knowledge and methodical assiduity.

The important question as to what relations exist between the number, quality and greatness of individual endowments and genius on the one side, and the character of a people on the other, is still unexplored and very obscure, although we possess a science which calls itself by the quite unjustified name of national psychology.

While on one side we have rarely made any serious study of national characteristics, but have confused them with achievements of culture and habits of life that mostly proceeded from a thin upper stratum alone, on the other we have as a rule tacitly set down individual endowment (with a strong emphasis on our own) as illustrations of national character. In this respect, too, we showed that laxity in proving what we wanted to prove which abounds everywhere from the point where calculation with things weighable and measurable leaves off, and judgment begins. We think it an established fact—in accordance with just this arbitrary test of genius—that genius belongs *par excellence* to the so-called blonde blue-eyed races of the earth. The fact that among the score or two of geniuses of all ages who have been determining forces in the world it is hardly possible to find a single example of this blue-blonde race, but they can be proved to have been almost all dark, did not affect the question. On the other hand the English, whose influence on culture has been surpassed by none, had their genius-forming power, in which they are actually deficient, seriously over-estimated. It was the reverse with the Jews. The fact that in spite of their small numbers they have produced more of world-moving genius than all other nations put together, and that from them has proceeded the whole transcendental ethics of the Western world, has not prevented their being pronounced wholly incapable of creative endowment.

We shall put aside all this rubbish and for the present decline to go into theoretic questions. Great individual endowments are related to national character—to the character of the mind, not that of the will, which must be considered apart—as the blossom to the plant or the crystal to the mother-solution; to determine the one from the other needs something more than a mechanical generalization. There is no such thing as a "race of thinkers and poets." This, however, we can say: that a people which begets great musicians, poets and philosophers is one which devotes itself to moods and to visions, while another, as for instance the Latin group, which creates forms and standards, is one that at the cost of mood and vision, incarnates its sense of will.

Devotion, receptivity, the feeling for Nature, comprehension, the passion for truth, meditative depth, spiritual love, are the fairest gifts that can be granted to any people, and to us they have been granted. But they exclude other gifts, which stand to-day in high repute, and which we affect in vain. They exclude the capacity for shaping forms and standards, the aptitude for rule, if not even for self-government; in any case the qualities which go to the creation of nationalities and civilizations.

It is no mere accident that in not one of the hundredfold provinces of life, from art to military organization, from State-craft to jointstock-companies, from saintliness to table-utensils, have we Germans discovered a single essential and enduring form. And again, there is scarcely one of these forms which we have not filled with a richer and more living content than those who first discovered it.

For whoever bears the All within himself can be satisfied with no form; he finds in himself at once vision and reality, thesis and antithesis. He seeks for a synthesis, but all form is one-sided. He conceives, chooses, comprehends, fulfils, breaks in pieces and throws away. He remains a unity in constant change, like the year as it proceeds day by day, hour by hour, and no two of them alike. He does not force things—out of respect for creation.

But he who makes forms must use force. He makes himself the standard and comprehends himself only. Everything else, everything that is extra-normal, unconformable, unintelligible and not understood remains for him something alien, trivial, inferior, or negligible. The maker of forms can rule, even by compulsion, without being a tyrant, for he is convinced of the value of what he brings and knows no doubts. He is ruthless, yet only up to a certain limit, which is determined by his sense of the inferiority of the other. The man who rejects forms, however, cannot rule; the very penetration into the domain of another seems to him a wrong to his own, the basis of which is recognition and allowance. If he is forced to penetrate, he loses all balance, for in wrong-doing he understands no gradations. Similarly he is incapable of civilizing, for he cannot take forms seriously; he violates them himself—how can he impose them upon others? In his inmost soul he is naïve, for creation is seething in him; but in execution he is conscious, critical, eclectic and methodical, in order that he may be completely master of the one-sided element into which he has forced himself. The man of forms, however, is, in his soul, rigid and conscious, but in action naïve, because he does not know the meaning of doubt.

Forms grow up like natural products in the course of centuries. They assume the existence of uniformity in individuals, fathers reproduced in sons with scarcely a variation. Egypt, Rome, and that modern land of antiquity, France, are examples. For generations France has been content with three architectural styles, which are really one and the same style. The changes in the language are hardly perceptible. The principal domestic utensils are almost the same as they were a hundred years ago, fashion is merely a vibration. Foreign living languages are little studied, their spirit is not understood, the pronunciation remains French. Foreign countries are looked on as a kind of menagerie; everything is measured by the native standard. Every one is a judge of everything, for he holds fast to the norm. Within the norm the French are keenly sensitive, their feeling for relations is very sure; the slightest deviation is observed. To doubt the validity of the norm is out of question; one might as well criticize the sun and moon as the style of Louis Quatorze.

The final judgment of the British in the affairs of life is "this is English," "that is not English." Foreign lands are a subject of geographical and ethnological study. The whole mighty will of a nation is here concentrated in the form of civilizing political energy. Every private inclination is a fad, and even fads have their fixed forms. An offence against table-manners is banned like an attack on the Church. Nature is mastered with consideration and intelligence, whether the problem is the breeding of sheep or the ruling of India.

The assurance, self-command and art of ruling which spring from forms are lacking in Germany. Our strongest spirits are formless; they are eclectic or titanic, whether they despise forms or choose forms or burst forms. We have three homes between which we hover—Germany, the earth, and heaven. We comprehend and honour everything—every land, every man, every art and every language; and we are fertilized by what is foreign; on the lower level we enjoy it and imitate it, on the higher it spurs us to creation. We are docile, and do not hate what rules and determines us, only what contracts us and makes us one-sided; an autocratic government may be tolerated, even venerated, if it knows how to be national and popular and does not interfere with our elbow-room.

We have already touched on the volitional character of the German people, a character which has been gravely altered by the subsidence of the ancient upper stratum of society, and by long privations and miseries. The Germans of Tacitus were a freedom-loving and turbulent people; of this not a trace is left. Any one who did not recognize under the autocracy that we care little for self-determination and self-responsibility may do so under the revolution, which merely arises out of an alteration in external conditions. We are not even yet a nation, but an association of interests and oppositions; a German *Irredenta*, as it has been and unfortunately will be shown, is an impossible conception. And since we are not a nation and represent no national idea, but only an association of households, it follows that our influence abroad can only be commercial, and not civilizing or propagandist.

From this side we are able to understand the German history of the past two centuries. Prussia, an extra-German Power, grown up in colonized territory, organized itself into a bureaucratic, feudal and military State. It succeeded in mastering half Germany and in loosely linking up the remainder. By rigid organization, by its federated Princes and by the strongest army in the world, it supplied the place of the national character and will which were wanting. Mechanism was pressed into the service, and bore the colossus into a period of blooming prosperity. The system looked like a nation; in reality it was an autocratic association of economic interests bristling with arms. It was incapable of developing national forces and ideas, not even in relation to its settlers in other lands; it was confined to commercial competition; weak alliances were relied on to secure the position externally; self-government was not granted, because the military organization was the pivot of the whole system; the drill-sergeant tone at home had its counterpart in the brusqueness of our foreign policy; enmities grew and organized themselves, and the catastrophe came.

For character of will we had substituted discipline. But discipline is not nationality; it is an external instrument, and when it breaks it leaves— nothing. Now since the Prussian system which called itself by the mediæval title of the German Empire was, in spite of the professors, no popular, national fabric, but a dynastic, military and compulsory association, with a constitutional façade, the interested nationalist elements took on the repulsive and dishonourable forms that we all know. The most deeply interested parties, cool and conscious of their strength, the Prussian representatives of the military and official nobility, avoided all declamation and only interfered when their interests were endangered. The greater industrialists sold themselves. A higher stratum of the middle-classes composed of certain circles of higher teachers and subaltern officials took the business seriously, and in order to escape from their drab existence created that atmosphere of hatred of Socialists, telegrams of homage, and megalomania, which made us intellectually and morally impossible before the world. Instead of the Germany of thought and spirit one saw suddenly a brutal, stupid community of interested persons, greedy for power, who gave themselves out as that Germany whose very opposite they were; who, unable to point to any achievements, any thought of their own, prided themselves on an imaginary race-unity which their very appearance contradicted; who had no ideas beyond rancour; the slaverings of league-oratory and subordination, and who with these properties, which they were pleased to call *Kultur*, undertook to bring blessing to the world.

It was no wonder; for our slavonicized association of interests, bent on subordination and on gain, does not produce ideas; its possessions were power, mechanism and money; whoever was impressed by these things believed they must impress others too, and so the conclusion was arrived at that all the great spirits of the past had lived only to make this triple combination supreme. Wagner had formed the bridge between the old Germany and the new—armoured cruisers and giant guns appeared as a free development from Kant and Hegel, and the word *Kultur*, a word which Germany ought to prohibit by law for thirty years to come, masked the confusion of thought.

To discover now, after our downfall, that Germany ought never to have carried on a continental let alone a world policy, would be a pitiful example of *esprit d'escalier*. It is true that it was our right, and even our duty, by our intellect, our ethics and our greatness, to carry it on; but the weakness of our character on the side of Will was the cause of its failure. Bismarck, a born realist in politics, grown up in the Prussian tradition, trained in the diplomatic tradition by Gortschakov, made the calamitous choice. He made us safe for certain decades; but it was only an intuitive policy in the manner of Stein that could have saved us for centuries.

In the midst of self-administered and self-determining nations the German people, from lack of self-consciousness, indolence of will and innate servility remained under a patriarchal system of government, a minor under tutelage of divinely-appointed dynasties and ruling classes. In the childish movement of the educated bourgeoisie of 1848 Bismarck saw only the helpless and Utopian, but not the symbolic side, which Marx might have shown him. His practical spirit judged with a smile that a handful of peasantry and grenadiers would suffice to bring to reason this dynastically-minded people. It was only too true; although the bulk of this people had not for thirty years been formed by the peasant class, and although he himself had learned how to make use of the power of the modern industrial State in peasant disguise. And so he refused to allow his countrymen to come of age; broke, with the superiority of genius, and with the weapons of success and authority, the incompetent forces that resisted him; created, by the magical mechanism of his Constitution, the German Empire as a mere continuation of the Prussian bureaucratic State reinforced, by the self-glorifying dynasties, with the whole volume of the still existing and justly appreciated habit of obedience; and annihilated for a generation every aspiration for freedom by branding it with the stain of moral and social depravity. Our political worthlessness and immaturity came to its climax in the race of office-climbers in 1880, which in 1900 gave place to the battle-fleet patriotism of the great capitalists.

A self-administered and a self-determining nation—such as the nations of the world, except ourselves, Austria and Russia, were, on the whole, at the turn of the century—would have been able to carry on a sound and steadfast policy in economics and public affairs, and to enjoy the confidence of the world, as little begrudged as America. On the other hand, a dangerous warship, armed upon an unexampled scale, given to backward movements and commanded by an uncontrollable sovran dilettante, could only expect sooner or later to be expelled from the harbour of the nations. History is apt to overdo it, especially when corruption has gone on too long; with every year that passed the doom became more certain; instead of being expelled, we were annihilated.

That four years of hunger, a lost war and a military revolt at last set us free, does not betoken any change of character; and when to-day a servile and facile Press lauds our wretched and idealess Constitution as the finest in the world, that gives us no assurance of its power to endure. Understanding is no substitute for character, but it is at any rate a step towards the goal; and if it is once understood that other measures are possible, and if, out of this period, certain writings and thoughts shall survive—and survive they will—then at any rate we may still be weak, but we shall be no longer blind.

It might be possible at the outset of our journey towards strength of will that we should grope our way slowly—very slowly—back to the old problems of power. It does not matter if we do. Before we get there, the world will be changed, and will be pregnant with new thoughts. Let us fulfil the duties for which Germany was made what it is. Let us go in quest of the idea and the faculty that are laid upon us; let us do this in order to live, to recover our health, to shape ourselves anew, to remain a People, to become a Nation, to create a future and to serve the world.

FOOTNOTES:

Geistigkeit. This is a difficult word to translate. It sometimes means merely intellectuality, sometimes in addition (as here) all that is implied in the phrase, "Ye know not what manner of spirit (οιου πνευματος) ye are of."

Referring to Werner Sombart's war-book, *Händler und Helden*.

Cf. Thomas Mann's remarkable book on the real significance of the war: *Betrachtungen eines Unpolitischen* (1918).

Sachlichkeit. Rathenau seems to have in mind the German feeling for disinterested study and research as illustrated, for instance, by the fact that when the German Government heard of the genius of Einstein they brought him to Berlin with a salary of nearly £1000 a year and no duties except to think. Modern bigotry has expelled him.

Where Kant lived and taught, and published his *Kritik der reinen Vernunft*.

As opposed to the inward, intellectual and spiritual character.

Stein was the chief leader of Prussia from the Frederician into the modern era. His ministry of reform by which a peasant-proprietary was established, and municipal institutions created, lasted only from September 1807 to November 1808.

X

ON balance it seems that the endowments of the German people work out as follows:—

High qualities of intellect and heart. Ethics and mentality normal. Originative will-power and independent activity, weak.

We give our devotion freely, and the heart rules in action. Our feelings are genuine and powerful. We have courage and endurance. Led by sentiment rather than by inspiration. We create no forms, are self-forgetful, seek no responsibility, obey rather than rule. In obedience we know no limit, and never question what is imposed upon us.

Of its own accord the German people would never have adopted an ideal of force. It was imposed on us by the idolaters of the great war-machine and those who gained by it; even Bismarck did not share it.

We are not competent to form an ideal of civilization, for the sense of unity, will to leadership, and formative energy are lacking to us. We have no political mission for the arrangement of other people's affairs, for we cannot arrange our own; we do not lead a full life, and are politically unripe.

We are endowed as no other people is for a mission of the spirit. Such a mission was ours till a century ago; we renounced it, because through political slackness of will-power we fell out of step; we did not keep pace with the other nations in internal political development, and, instead, devoted ourselves to the most far-reaching developments of mechanism and to their counterpart in bids for power. It was Faust, lured away from his true path, cast off by the Earth-Spirit, astray among witches, brawlers and alchemists.

But the Faust-soul of Germany is not dead. Of all peoples on the earth we alone have never ceased to struggle with ourselves. And not with ourselves alone, but with our dæmon, our God. We still hear within ourselves the All, we still expand in every breath of creation. We understand the language of things, of men and of peoples. We measure everything by itself, not by us; we do not seek our own will, but the truth. We are all alike and yet all different; each of us is a wanderer, a brooder, a seeker. Things of the spirit are taken seriously with us; we do not make them serve our lives, we serve them with ours.

"And you dare to say this, in the face of all the brutalizing and bemiring that we experience—the profiteering and gormandizing, the abject submissiveness, the shameless desertions, the apathy, the insincerity, the heartlessness and mindlessness of our day?"

Yes, I dare to say it, for I believe it and I know it. The soul of the German people lies still in the convulsions and hallucinations of its slow recovery. It is recovery not alone from the war, but from something worse, its hundred-years' alienation from itself. The much-ridiculed choice of our old romantic unheraldic colours, black, red and gold, instead of the bodiless and soulless colours under which we waged the war, was, among the whirling follies of the time, a faint symbolic movement of our better mind. We must reunite ourselves with the days before we ceased to be Germans and became Berliners.

What we need is Spirit. The whole world needs it, no more and no less than we do, but will never create it. History knows why it decided for Versailles and the Hall of Mirrors. Not mechanism alone, with its retinue of nationalism and imperialism, is now again and for the last time to be glorified; no, the whole Franco-British policy of acquisition mounts up even to the throne of the Sun-king, and it is seriously believed that it will govern the destinies of the world for centuries to come. An inconceivable, and, in its monstrous irony, unsurpassable drama, which is put forward as the introduction to the great era. The bourgeois conscience of the West has no inkling of what it means. To this conscience, the war was a huge violation of decency, contrived by bandits; its victory is the final triumph of a capitalist, rationalistic civilization; the torch lit in the East means murder and incendiarism, and the upward migration of the people from the depths is to it invisible.

No; it is not here that the spirit of the future is being formed. One may discover further ingenious devices, lightning-conductors to mitigate the stroke; but gently or violently a natural force will have its way, and the new earth which it is preparing needs new seed.

That we have been given the faculty to shape a new spirit does not imply that we are at liberty to choose whether we shall do it or not. Even if it were not for our life's sake—even if it were against our life—still we must obey. But it *is* for our life's sake, as we have seen, and as it is indeed obvious, for every organism can live only by fulfilling the purpose of its being.

And now we have got to a very dangerous place—a place where the usual moral peroration lies in wait for us—that German peroration which announces universal redemption, and immediately, on that lofty note, closes the discussion. Fatherland, Morality, Humanity, Labour, Courage, Confidence—we all know how it goes, the writer has written something fine, the reader has read something fine; emotion on both sides, little conviction on either.

It appears, then, that I have just been writing something extremely suspect. Has the reader followed me through five-and-thirty of these difficult folios in order to arrive in the end at that very everyday term, Spirit? Is there any term in commoner use, and what are we to think about it? Softly—there is worse to come! The next word is still more dubious, philistinishly so, in fact—the word Culture. I cannot help it—we must pass on by way of these everyday conceptions. We must get through the crowd, where hack-phrases elbow us. Any journey you may take, though it were to Tibet, must begin at the Berlin Central Railway Station. What is wrong with these popular phrases is not that they start from an everyday conception, but that they remain content with it, and do not think it out to the end.

Our task, therefore, stated in the most general terms, is to make actually spiritual a people which is capable of spirituality. And since spirituality cannot be propped up by any external thrust, by sermons, newspaper articles, leagues, or propaganda, but must be associated with life and developed out of life, so the organic process and the condition of life to which it leads is called Culture.

It is only with deep reluctance and after long search that I have written down this beautiful word, a word now worn almost beyond recognition. Can we find our way back to its application and significance? Even when it is not drawn out with a futile prefix one can hardly detect its pure meaning by reason of the many overtones. The school, if possible the university, some French and English, the rules about I and Me, visiting-cards, shirt-cuffs, foreign phrases, top-hats, table-manners: these are some of the overtones that make themselves heard when we talk of a cultured man, or rather as they have it a cultured gentleman. A hundred years ago, as the word implies, we understood by culture the unfolding and the full possession of innate bodily, spiritual and moral forces. In this sense Goethe showed us the two fraternal figures formed after his own image: Faust the richer, and the poorer Wilhelm Meister, striving for culture.

The ideal which hovers before us is not one of education, not even one of knowledge, although both education and knowledge enter into it; it is an ideal of the Will. It will not be easy to convey the breadth and the boundless range which we are to attach to this conception. That it is not an airy figment is clear from the fact that for centuries the Greeks, with full consciousness, adopted as their highest law (though directed to a somewhat different end) that impulse of the will which they called *Kalokagathia*.

From one who has introduced the conception of mechanism into German thought, who has rescued the conception of the soul from the hands of the psychologists and brought it back to its primal meaning, who has written so much about soulless intellectualism, and has put forward the empire of the soul as the goal of humanity, it is not to be expected that he should preach any mechanical kind of culture, or indeed any that it is possible to acquire by learning.

How culture is to be produced we shall see; the first thing necessary is that it should be willed.

Willed it must be, in a sense and with a strength of purpose and a force of appreciation of which we to-day, when the ages of faith, of the Reformation, of the German classics, and the wars of liberation, lie so far behind us, have no idea at all.

When the current conception of intellectual culture so much prized in family, society and business life, and tricked out with criticisms of style, with historical data and incidents of travel is justly ridiculed, then the will to complete cultivation of the body, the intellect and the soul of the people must be so strong that all questions of convenience, of enjoyment, of prestige and of material interests must sink far into the background. This word must sound so that all who hear it can look in each other's eyes with a full mutual understanding and without the slightest sense of ambiguity; just as they do in Japan when the name of the common head of all families, the Mikado, is named. There must be one thing in Germany and it must be this thing, which is altogether out of reach of the yawning, blinking and grinning scepticism of the coffee-house, and of the belching and growling of the tavern. Any man who puts this thing aside in favour of his class-ideas, or his speculations in lard, or his dividends, or the demands of his Union, must understand that he is doing something as offensive as if he went out in public without washing himself.

The conception of Culture as our true and unique faculty must be so profoundly grasped that in public life and legislation it must have the first word and the last. Though we become as poor as church-mice we must stake our last penny on this, and tune up our education and instruction, our models and outlook, our motives and claims, our achievement and our atmosphere, to so high a point that any one coming into Germany shall feel that he is entering into a new age.

Society must be penetrated by this conception. Those classes which already possess something resembling it—such as training, education, experience, tradition, outlook, good breeding—must pour out with both hands what they have to dispense; not in the way of endowments, conventicles, lectures and patronizing visits, but in quiet, self-sacrificing, personal service.

All this, of course, cannot be done without the free response of the other side. The devoted attempts which have been made, especially in England, and for some years with us too, to win this response by long and unselfish solicitation were destined to remain merely the mission of individual lives, for they were not supported by the will of the community as a whole; it rather ran counter to them. A Peace of God must be proclaimed, not as between the Haves and the Have-nots, not between the proletariat and the capitalists, not between the so-called cultured classes and the uncultured, but between those who are ready for a mutual exchange of experience, a give-and-take of their tradition on both sides. Not an exchange on business principles, such as propaganda in satisfaction of demands, or curiosity on one side for a new pastime on the other, but a covenant. This, however, is only practicable if the class-war, as an end in itself, is put a stop to.

The great change itself cannot be come by so cheaply; it demands other assumptions, of which we shall have something to say later. But the attitude and temper, the recognition of the task, could not be better introduced than through the mutual service of the two social strata.

We have still at our disposal, handed on from the past, certain organized methods of investigation and administration. We now need chairs and institutes of research, not for the trivial business of popular enlightenment and lectures, but for the study and investigation of the needs of national culture, the idea which must now take the place of national defence. We shall have need of central authorities, not, like the late Ministries of Culture skimping the scanty endowment of the Board Schools, but doing the work of German education, progress, and interchange of labour.

FOOTNOTES:

Black, red and gold were originally the colours of a students' Corps in Frankfort. They were adopted as the colours of the abortive German Federation of 1848, apparently under a mistaken idea that they represented the colours of the ancient Germanic Empire. The colours of the Empire of 1870 were the Prussian black and white, with the addition of red.

Geist.

Bildung. It is as difficult in English as it is in German to render in one word exactly what the author is thinking of. In its literal sense Bildung implies a shaping and formative action.

Ausbildung.

A harmony of character, compounded of beauty and goodness.

Arbeitsausgleich. The meaning of this will be apparent later.

———

XI

SOME decades ago the conscience of middle-class society in England was stirred. The result was Toynbee Hall and the Settlements-movement, which afterwards found praiseworthy counterparts in Germany. Society had begun to understand the wrong which it had done to its brothers, the proletariat, whom it had robbed of mind, and offered them instead soul-destroying, mechanical labour. Then choice spirits arose who dedicated their whole lives to the service of their brothers. This great and noble work did much to soften pain and hatred, and here and there many a soul was saved by it; but it could not act as it was intended to act, because it could not become what it imagined itself to be.

It ought to have been, and believed itself to be, a simple and obvious piece of love-service, a pure interchange of spiritual possessions between class and class, no condescending pity or educative mission. It was a noble and a splendid error; the movement retained the form of sacrifice and benefaction. On both sides social feeling was indifferent to it, or even hostile. What one hand gave, a thousand others took back; what one hand received, a thousand others rejected. The collective conscience of a class had never been stirred, it was merely that the conscience of certain members of upper-class society had sent out envoys; it had not moved as a body. Individuals were ready to sacrifice themselves, but the conditions of labour remained unchanged.

So long as a general wrong is allowed to stand, it gives the lie to every individual effort. The wrong becomes even more bitter because it loses its unconsciousness—men know it for wrong, and do not amend it. For this reason a second movement of importance, that of the People's High Schools, which has created in Denmark the most advanced peasant-class in existence, can achieve no social reform in lands cloven by proletarianism. If in addition to this the High School movement should depart from its original conception, that of a temporary community of life between the teachers and the taught, and should, instead of this, resolve itself into a lecture-institution, then the danger arises that what is offered will be disconnected matter, intended for entertainment, and without any basis of real knowledge, something commonly called half-culture which is worse than unculture, and is more properly described as misculture.

No work of the charitable type can bring about the reconciliation of classes or be a substitute for popular education. The reconciliation of classes, however, even if it were attainable, is by no means our goal, but rather the abolition of classes, and our ultimate object is not popular education but popular culture. We do not intend to give with one hand and take back with the other, we shall not condemn a brother-people to dullness and quicken a few chosen individuals; no, we mean to go to the root of the evil, to break down the monopoly of culture, and to create a new people, united and cultured throughout.

But the root of the trouble lies in the conditions of labour. It is an idle dream to imagine that out of that soulless subdivision of labour which governs our mechanical methods of production, the old handicrafts can ever be developed again. Short of some catastrophic depopulation which shall restore the mediæval relation between the area of the soil and the numbers that occupy it, the subdivision of labour will have to stand, and so long as it stands no man will complete his job from start to finish—he will only do a section of it; at best, and assuming the highest mechanical development, it will be a work of supervision. But mindless and soulless work no man can do with any joy. The terrible fact about the mechanization of industry is that productive work, the elementary condition of life, the very form of existence, which fills more than half of each man's waking day, is by it made hated and hateful. It degrades the industrious man, thrilling with energy, into a work-shy slacker—for what else does it mean that all social conflicts culminate in the demand for a shortening of the hours of work? For the peasant, the research-worker, the artist, the working day is never long enough; for the artisan, who calls himself *par excellence* a "worker," it can never be too short.

The advance of technical invention will make it possible in the end to transform all mechanical work into supervision. But the process will be long and partial, we cannot wait till it is completed, especially as times will come when technical knowledge will stand still, or even, it may be, go back. Any one who knows in his own flesh what mechanical work is like, who knows the feeling of hanging with one's whole soul on the creeping movement of the minute-hand, the horror that seizes him when a glance at the watch shows that the eternity which has passed has lasted only ten minutes, who has had to measure the day's task by the sound of a bell, who kills his lifetime, hour after hour, with the one longing that it might die more quickly—he knows how the shortening of the working day, whatever may be put in its place, has become for the factory artisan a goal of existence.

But he knows something else as well. He knows the deadliest of all wearinesses—the weariness of the soul. Not the rest when one breathes again after wholesome bodily exertion, not the need for relaxation and distraction after a great effort of intellect, but an empty stupor of exhaustion, like the revulsion after unnatural excess. It is the shallowest kind of tea-table chatter to talk about good music, edifying and instructive lectures, a cheerful walk in God's free Nature, a quiet hour of reading by the lamp, and so on, as a remedy for this. Drink, cards, agitation, the cinemas, and dissipation can alone flog up the mishandled nerves and muscles, until they wilt again under the next day's toil.

The worker has no means of comparison. He does not know what wholesome labour feels like. He will never find his way back to work on the land, for there he cannot get the counter-poisons which he thinks indispensable, and he lacks the organic, ordering mind which mechanical employment has destroyed. Even if some did get back, it would be in vain, for though agriculture is hungering for thousands of hands it cannot absorb millions. The worker has no means of comparison; hence his bottomless contempt for intellectual work, the results of which he recognizes, but which, in regard to the labour it costs, he puts on a level with the idling of the folk whom he sees strolling or driving about with their lapdogs in the fashionable streets.

The middle-class conscience, and even that of the men of science, turns away its face in shameful cowardice from the horror of mechanized labour. Apart from the well-meaning æsthetes who live in rural elegance surrounded by all the appliances which mechanism can supply, who wrinkle their brows when the electric light goes out, and who write pamphlets asking with pained surprise why people cannot return to the old land-work and handicraft, most of us take mechanical labour as an unalterable condition of life, and merely congratulate ourselves that it is not we who have to do it.

The Utopianist agitators who knowingly or unknowingly suppress the essential truth that their world of equality will be a world of the bitterest poverty, treat the situation just as lightly. Before them, in the future State, hovers the vision of some exceptional literary or political appointment. The others may console themselves with the thought that in spite of a still deeper degree of poverty, towards which they are sinking by their own inactivity, the hell of mechanical work, by no means abolished, will probably be a little reduced, so far as regards the time they spend in it. The notion that mechanical work will be made acceptable and reconciled with intellectual, if only it is short enough and properly paid, has never been thought out; it is a still-born child of mental lethargy, like all those visions of the future that are being held up to our eyes. Try notions like this on any other ill—toothache, for instance! All our rhetoric about mechanical work being no ill at all, is ignorant or fraudulent, and if nothing further be done than to reduce it to four hours, all our social struggles will immediately be concentrated on bringing it down to two. The goal of Socialism, so far as it relates to this *pons asinorum* of shortening hours, is simply the right to loaf.

Let us look facts in the face. Mechanical work is an evil in itself, and it is one which we never can get rid of by any conceivable economic or social transformation. Neither Karl Marx nor Lenin has succeeded here, and on this reef will be wrecked every future State that may be set up on the basis of current Socialistic ideas. In this point lies the central problem of Socialism; undisturbed, as was till lately that legendary conception of surplus-value, and bedded, like that conception, in a rats'-nest of rhetorical phrases, repeated from mouth to mouth and never tested by examination.

The bringing of Mind into the masses, the cultured State, which is the only possible foundation of a society worthy of humanity, must remain unattainable until everything conceivable has been thought out and done to alleviate the mischievous operation of this evil, which dulls and stupefies the human spirit and which, in itself, is ineradicable. No Soviet-policy, no socialization, no property-policy, no popular education, nor any other of the catchwords which form *ad nauseam* the monotonous staple of our current discussion of affairs, can go to the heart of the problem. Instead we must establish and put into practice the principle which I have called that of the Interchange of Labour, and which I must now, in broad outline, endeavour to explain.

The object of this principle is to bring mind into labour. It demands— since mind cannot be brought into mechanical work beyond a certain degree fixed by technical conditions—that the day's work as a whole shall have a share of it, by means of the exchange and association of mental and mechanical employment. Until this principle shall have been carried into effect, all true culture of the people remains impossible. So long as there is no culture of the people, so long must culture remain a monopoly of the classes, and of escapes from the masses; so long must society be wanting in equilibrium, a union open to breach from every side, and one which, however highly its social institutions may be developed, holds down the people to forced labour, and destroys culture.

FOOTNOTES:

Bildungsstaat.

XII

THERE is a way by which the day's work can be ennobled, and even have mind brought into it, on capitalistic lines. Before the War we were just about to enter on this path—America is treading it now. Its fundamental condition is a huge increase in general well-being.

The daily wages of the American working-man have risen, as we have already remarked, to seven or even ten dollars, corresponding to a purchasing power of over a hundred marks. This amounts to so radical a removal of all restrictions in domestic economy that one can no longer speak of the proletarian condition as existing in the United States. A man who drives to his work in his own automobile can satisfy all his reasonable needs in the way of recreation and of extending his education, he looks at his sectional job (as has not seldom been the case in America even in earlier days) with a critical eye, he forms his own judgment of its place in the whole, he improves the processes, and amuses himself by being both workman and engineer. (Consider in the light of this fact the value of the prophecy that America is standing on the brink of Bolshevism!)

In a country whose wealth at this moment—in consequence of war-profits and depreciation of money—is almost equal to that of the rest of the world put together, the process of abolishing proletarianism can go forward on capitalistic lines. But we Germans, since it is decreed that we shall be among the poorest of the peoples, and must begin afresh, and live for the future—we shall renounce without envy the broad path of the old way of thought, the way of riches, in order to clear with hard work the new path on which, one day, all will have to follow us. The way of Culture is the way to which we are pointed, and we have described Interchange of Labour as the fundamental condition which enables us to travel it. It is now clear that the conception of popular culture is not, after all, represented by any of the five-and-twenty idealizing catchwords with which we are wont to console ourselves in our elegiac orations, but that by it is meant a clearly defined political procedure.

By the principle of Interchange of Labour it is required that every employee engaged in mechanical work can claim to do a portion of his day's work in intellectual employment; and that every brainworker shall be obliged to devote a portion of his day to physical labour.

There are, of course, fixed limits to the application of this principle, on the one side in intellectual, on the other in bodily incapacity, as well as in those rare cases where it is recognized that the interrupted hours of intellectual work cannot be made good.

We would also establish a year of Labour-Service, to be devoted by the whole youth of Germany, of both sexes, to bodily training and work.

The tests of capacity and of the claim to be reckoned as "cultured" is not to consist in examinations but in proof of work. Any one who can offer some show of claim can demand to be tested, and, if the result is favourable, to receive further culture. Thus we shall be taking seriously the question of the ascent to higher grades, which, so long as it depends on a particular age, or on school certificates, must remain on paper.

Let no one say that this testing system is a mere mechanical method, that it degrades Culture from its intellectual dignity, and is equivalent to the Chinese literary tests for office. True culture is distinguished from mere sybaritic æstheticism in that in some sense or other it makes for production. Where there is no talent for art or for creative thought, then there remain to be developed the educational forces of judgment, or a faculty for the conduct of life, which must have their influence.

Different categories of Culture will arise of themselves; not ranks or castes or classes, but grades of society, each of which may be attained by any one. No one must be able to say that any monopoly of culture has barred his way, or that training and testing have been denied him. If the culture be genuine it will never look down in intellectual arrogance on the stages below it; if it have duties associated with it, then he who has rejected the path of ascent, or has failed in it, cannot claim to fulfil those duties. Any one who has no faculty but that of a glib tongue will find in the multiplicity of callings some field for his activity; but the rule of the talker, backed by force or not, will at any rate be spared us.

At this point we may hear a voice from the average heart of Socialism exclaim: "How is this? Do you call that having no castes? We have just begun to shake off the yoke of the capitalists and now are we expected to put the cultured in command? This is pure reaction!"

Softly! If this is a case of misunderstanding, we shall clear it up. If any scruples still remain, we shall consider them further.

Let us take the misunderstanding first. It is apparently forgotten that capitalism ruled by hereditary power. Any one who belonged to that circle ruled along with it, whether he were competent to rule or not. But culture is not a heritable possession; no one can win it save by virtue of a higher spirit and will. He who has this spirit and this will, can and will win it. He who wins it is fit for higher responsibilities. Is the voice from the average heart answered?

No. It replies: "Heritable or not, what do we care? We are out for equality. Distinctions in culture are a kind of aristocracy."

Now, good heart, you have revealed yourself. What was the meaning of your everlasting talk about the ladder for the rise of capacity? I shall tell you. The capable man is to toil, and to rise just so far as you permit him, namely, till you can possess yourselves of the fruits of his labour: then he is to be thrust down, and the loudest mouth is to rule. You are not pleased with this interpretation? Neither am I, so we are quits.

For of the folly of imagining a society of equals I do not intend to speak. The average man, who cannot understand equality of human dignity, equality before God, thinks nothing of demanding equality in externals, equality in responsibility and vocation. But this sham equality is the enemy of the true, for it does not fit man's burden to his strength, it creates overburdened, misused natures, driving the one to scamped work and hypocrisy, and the other to cynicism. Every accidental and inherited advantage must indeed be done away with. But if there is any one who, among men equal in external conditions, in duties and in claims, demands that they should also be equal in mind, in will and in heart—let him begin by altering Nature!

In remuneration also, that is to say, in the apportionment of conditions of work, a mechanical equality would be tantamount to an unjust and intolerable inequality in the actual distribution or remission of work. Work of the highest class, creative and intellectual work—the most self-sacrificing that is known to man because it draws to itself and swallows up a man's whole life, including his hours of leisure and recreation—this work demands extreme consideration, in the form of solitude, freedom from disturbance, from trivial and distracting cares or occupations, and contact with Nature. This kind of consideration is, from the economic point of view, an outlay which mechanical work does not require. If mechanical and intellectual work are to be placed under the same specific conditions, under which the highest standard of output is to be maintained and the producers are as far as possible to bear an equal burden, then the scale of remuneration must be different. Starting from a subsistence minimum it must for intellectual work be graded two stages upward, one for the output, and one for the grade of culture implied.

Women will also be subject to this system of grading whether they exercise any vocation outside their homes or not, for society has a deep interest in the culture of its mothers, and in external incentives to culture women must share equally with men.

An intimate sense of association will grow up within each grade of culture. This, however, will not impair the general solidarity of the people, since no hereditary family egoism can arise. This sense of association, renewed with elements that vary from generation to generation, and corresponding very much to the relations between contemporary artists who spring from different classes or territories, will dissolve the relics of the old hereditary sentiment and absorb into itself whatever traditional values the latter may possess.

Between the separate grades there will not only be the connexion afforded by the living possibilities of free ascent from one to the other, but the system of ever-renewed co-operation in rank-and-file at the same work will in itself promote culture, tradition, and the consciousness of union. We need only recall the old gilds and military associations in order to realize what a high degree of manly civic consciousness can arise from the visible community of duty and achievement. The mechanical worker will become the instructor of his temporary comrade and guest, and the latter will in turn widen the other's outlook, and emulate him in the development of the processes of production. The manual worker will bring to the desk and the board-room his freedom from prepossessions and the practical experience of his calling; he will learn how to deal with abstractions and general ideas; he will gain a respect for intellectual work, and will feel the impulse to win new knowledge and faculty, or to make good what he has neglected.

Two objections remain to be considered and confuted.

First: there are far more places to be filled in mechanical than in intellectual employment. Is it possible so to organize the interchange of work that every one who desires intellectual employment can find it? The answer is: that, whether we like it or not, all work tends more and more to take on an administrative character. Just as in industry there is ever more talk and less production, so our economic life is working itself out through thousands upon thousands of new organizations. Industrial Councils, Councils of Workers, Gild-Councils, are forming themselves in among the existing agencies of administration; and the immediate consequence of this is a tremendous drop in production, to be followed later by a more highly articulated and more remunerative system of work. It is as if a marble statue came to life, and then had to be internally equipped with bones, muscles, veins and nerves. Or it resembles the transformation of a shabby piece of suburban building-ground: it has to be dug up, drained, paved, fenced; and until traffic has poured into it, it remains a comfortless and dismal waste.

But the administrative side of our future economic and national life demands the creation of so many posts of intellectual work that at present there is not the trained *personnel* to fill it. If the Year of Labour-Service is introduced, there will be still more defections and gaps to be filled. The rush for intellectual work is more likely to be too small than too great.

Let us come to the second objection. Will not confusion be worse confounded if there are many who have to fill two jobs, if, in these jobs constant exchanges are taking place, if the periods of work are brief and subject to untimely interruptions, if time and work are lost through never-ending rearrangement?

Assuredly. And any one who starts with the idea of the old high-strung work done, as it were, under military discipline, any one who cherishes the remotest idea that this system can ever return, in spite of the fact that its clamps and springs have been dashed to pieces, may well lament these unsettlements. One who starts from the fluctuating conditions of our present-day, make-believe labour will take organic unsettlements as part of the price to be paid, if they only lead in the end to systematic production. But one who weighs the fact that the make-believe life of our present economy has not even yet reached its final form, will discern in every new transition-form, however tedious, the final redemption; in so far, at least, as any equilibrium is capable of being restored at all.

The essence of the interchange of labour will, therefore, consist in this, that while the distinction between physical and intellectual work will still exist, there will be no distinction between a physical and intellectual calling. Until advanced age may forbid, it will be open to every man not merely to acquire some ornamental branches of knowledge but seriously and with both feet to take his footing in the opposite calling to his own.

The different callings will learn to know and respect each other, and to understand their respective difficulties. This applies particularly to those who call themselves the operative workers.

As soon as hereditary idleness has come to an end and loafing has been trampled out, then many a one, who now thinks that mental work is mere chattering, will learn through his novitiate at the desk, that thinking hurts. If he does not feel himself equal to this kneading and rummaging of the brain, he will go back with relief to his workshop; he will neither envy nor despise those who are operative workers with the brain, and will understand, or at least unconsciously feel, the oppositions in human nature and the differences in conditions of life, and will know them to be just. He cannot and must not keep himself wholly aloof from the elements of mental training; his contact with brainworkers will not cease; and thus his complete and passive resignation to the domination of ignorant rhetoric will lose its charm.

Any man will be respected who contents himself with the lowest prescribed measure of culture, who modestly renounces further study, and goes back to manual work. But there will be no excuse for those who know nothing and can do nothing, but pretend to set everybody right; for there will be no monopoly of culture to keep them down, and all genuine faculty must come to the test of action.

To-day there are three classes of social swindlers. First, those who live on the community without returning it any service. These are the people who live idly on inherited money, and the loafers. Against these social legislation must be framed. Secondly, those who deliberately practise "ca' canny," and therefore live on the surplus work of their fellows. These are the champions of the principle: Every one according to his need, no one according to his deed; the *saboteurs* of labour. Against these the remedy lies in the spread of intelligence and a just system of remuneration. Thirdly, there are those who simulate thought and brain-work while they have nothing to give but hack phrases uttered with a glib tongue. Against these worst of all swindlers, these sinners against the Spirit, the remedy is culture.

And this, in the new Order, is open to every one, young or old, who can maintain his foothold in the exercise of intellect, when the chance is offered him. He who in his test-exercise reaches a normal standard of accomplishment can demand that he shall not be sent back to manual work, but continue to be employed in the same occupation, and be further cultivated in whatever direction he desires. At every further stage of development a corresponding sphere of activity is to be opened to him, up to the point at which the limits of his capacity come into sight.

Let no one object that the rush for intellectual work will become uncontrollable. Would that it might! For then the country would be so highly developed and its methods of work so perfected that there would be quite a new relation between the demand for head-work and for hand-work. For a long time to come this rush will be far smaller than we imagine; for the immediate future it will suffice if the rising forces are set free, and the laggard are tranquillized.

But, the Radicals will cry, what an unsocial principle! Have we at last, with difficulty, brought it to the point that the accursed one-year examination is abrogated, and now are we again to be condemned according to this so-called standard of culture?

Stay! there is a fallacy here. In our transition period which is still quite dominated by the monopoly of culture, I have nothing to say against the abrogation of every educational test, even though in a few years we shall feel the deeply depressing effects which will arise from the domination of the uncultured.

But the transition period will come to an end. Then every one who likes will be able to learn and to execute, and every one who is able will wish to do so.

"But supposing one does not wish? May not he be the very one who is most capable of achievement? We don't want model pupils."

Nor do I want model pupils. The boy who has learnt nothing may make his trial as a man when culture is open to all. But if, as a man, he does not care to rack his brains he will be thought none the less of; he will merely be offered ordinary work according to his choice.

But those who wish to see responsibility and the destiny of the country placed in the hands of men who do not care to rack their brains, must not entrench themselves behind social principles, but plainly admit that they want for all time to establish the rule of demagogy and the vulgarization of intellect. It is not for such a one to pass judgment on the mission of Germany.

The way to the German mission, to German culture, which is to be no more a culture of the classes but of the people, stands open to all by means of the Interchange of Labour. The whole land is as it were a single ship's crew; the issues are the same for all. The manual worker is no longer kept down by over-fatigue, and the brainworker is no longer cut off from the rest of the people.

The manual worker no longer regards the territory of culture as a sort of inaccessible island, but rather as a district which he can visit every day and in which he is quite at home. Every one in future will start even in school training, and the degree to which his further culture may be carried will not be limited by want of money or of time, or, above all, of opportunity. He will continually have intercourse with men of culture, and in that intercourse he will at once give and receive; the habits of thought, the methods and the range of intellectual work which are now only the heritage of a few will be his own; and the twofold language of the country, the language of conceptions and the language of things, will for him be one.

There will be no permanent system of stratification; the energies of the people, rising and falling, will be in constant movement and their elements will never lose touch. There may be self-tormenting and unhappily constituted natures who will hate their own dispositions and the destiny they have shaped for themselves—these aberrations will never cease so long as men are men—but there will be no more hatred of class for class, any more than there is in any voluntary association of artists or of athletes.

And since culture is to be at once the recognized social aim of the country and the personal goal and standard of each individual, the struggle for possessions and enjoyments, doubly restrained by public opinion and by deeper insight, will sink into the background.

But the spirit of the land will not resemble any that we know at present. As in the Middle Ages, a spiritual power will rule, but it will not be imposed from without or above, it will be a creation from within. The competition of all will be like that of the best in the time of the Renaissance, but it will not be a competition for conventional values but for the furthering of life. The country will become, as it was in former days, a generous giver, not, however, from the lofty eminence of a class set apart, but out of the whole strength of the people.

Again, for the first time, the convinced and conscious will of a people will be seen to direct itself to a common and recognized goal. This is a fact of immeasurable significance, it implies the exercise of forces which we only discern on the rare mountain-peaks of history, and of which the last example was the French Revolution.

But those dangers of which we have spoken, that hell of a mechanical socialism, of institutions and arrangements without sentiment or spirit, are done away with, for production has ceased to be merely material and formal, it has acquired absolute value and substance. Spirit is the only end that sanctifies all means; and it sanctifies not by justifying them but by purifying them.

FOOTNOTES:

Vergeistigt werden. It is difficult to render this word in the sense in which Rathenau uses it; 'intellectualized' does not say enough, and 'spiritualized' says a little too much.

Assuming that the highest output is reached in the particular instance which of course will not be the case with every worker whether in the mechanical or intellectual sphere. The author appears to be referring to amount, not quality, of output, as the latter would be covered by the second clause, relating to grade of culture (Bildungsstufe).

Referring to the shortening of military service which used to be accorded to recruits of a certain educational standard.

XIII

AS the kinsfolk of a dying man comfort themselves in the death-chamber with every little droop in the curve of temperature, although they know in their hearts that the hour has come, so our critics flatter themselves with the idea that in the end all will come right, if not by itself at least with trifling exertion. But it is not so: except by the greatest exertion nothing will come right. Our lake-city of economics and social order is ripe for collapse, for the piles on which it is built are decayed. It is true that it still stands, and will be standing for an hour or so, and life goes on in it very much as in the days when it was sound. We can choose either to leave it alone, and await the downfall of the city, among whose ruins life will never bloom again, or we can begin the underpinning of the tottering edifice, a process which will last for decades, which will allow no peace to any of us, which will be toilsome and dangerous, and will end almost imperceptibly, when the ancient city has been transformed into the new.

Let us have no doubt about it: something tremendous and unprecedented has to be accomplished here. Does any thinking man believe that when the social order of the world has collapsed, when a country of the importance of Germany has lost the very basis of its existence, when the development of centuries is broken off, its faculties and its traditions emptied of value and repudiated—does any man really believe that by means of certain clauses in a Constitution a few confiscations, socializations and rises in wages, a nation of sixty millions can be endowed with a new historical reason for existence? Why is not the negro republic of Liberia ahead of all of us?

Our character is weak on the side of will, and our former lords say that we are good for nothing except under strict discipline administered by dynasts and hereditary nobles. If that is true, it is all over with us; unless some dictator shall take pity on us and give us a modest place among the nations with a great past and a small future. If we are worthy of our name we must be born again of the Spirit. Merely to conceive this is in itself an achievement for a people; to carry it out, to embody the conception in a new order of society, is at once a test and an achievement.

Our social ethics must take up a new position. Hitherto—stripping off the usual rhetorical phrases—it has taken its stand on two effective and really driving principles, those of Duty and of Success; two side-views of Individualism. All else, including love of one's neighbour, sense of solidarity, faith, spiritual cultivation, feeling for Nature, was (apart from a few lofty spirits) merely subsidiary; means to an end, convention or falsehood. There were few whose careers were not influenced by these estimates; the majority of the upper classes was wholly under their dominion.

The two goals of our wishes, to have something and to be something, were expressed by the whole outward aspect of society. The great object was not to be counted as a Tom, Dick or Harry, one who had less, or was less, than others. There were grades of being, grades of human being: it was possible to be something, to be much, to be little, or to be nothing at all. From the white collar to the pearl necklace, from the good nursery to the saloon car, from the watch-ribbon to the sword-belt, from the place at the ordinary to the title of Excellency, everything was a proof of what one had, or was, or believed oneself to be. If one did not know a man one must not speak to him; if one knew him, one might borrow a hundred marks from him, but one must not ask him for a penny. Whoever had wealth displayed it in order to be admired; whoever had a social position displayed his unapproachability and the weight of his dignity, as, for instance, when with an absent look and lost in the burden of his own existence he entered a dining-hall. From inferiors one demanded a degrading attitude and forms of speech, and presented to them a face of stone; towards those in higher position one came to life and displayed an attentive civility. It was—or shall we say is?—permissible to lavish in an hour the monthly income of a poor family. "One had it to spend" and "what business was it of theirs?" In the lower ranks there was much of genuine revolt against these abuses and also much envy and malice, much open imitation, and much of secret admiration. Every silly craze was cheapened in hideous imitations, the suburb and the village made a display which in quality, indeed, fell below the model, but in quantity not at all.

It may be said that these were excrescences or city fashions; that one must not generalize. These are empty phrases. To understand the spirit of a society it is not hermits that one must study. And, moreover, let any one ask himself whether this society was really based on the idea of solidarity and human friendliness or upon unscrupulous personal interests and exploitation, on shows and shams, on the demand for service and the claim to command. If anything can explain the eagerness with which we Germans flung ourselves into a war whose origins we did not know and did not want to know, then besides the conscious objects, advantage, rehabilitation, and renown, we must also take into account the obscure impulse of the national conscience which in the midst of evil individualism and of personal and class egoism yearned for the sense of solidarity and fusion.

Is it objected that all this lies deeply rooted in human nature, that it has been there from time immemorial, and it is impossible to alter it at one stroke? Pedantic drivel! Many things lie deep in human nature, and it depends on which of these the will chooses to develop. And who talked of altering things at one stroke? Our judgment of values is to be transformed, and if human nature never changed, much that now flaunts itself in the sunshine would be creeping in the shade. This transformation of judgment is a matter of recognizing things for what they are. When pomp, extravagance, exclusiveness, frivolity and fastness, greed, place-hunting and vulgar envy are looked on with the same eyes as aberrations in other provinces of life, then we shall not indeed have abolished all vice, but the atmosphere will be purified. Look at our sturdy Socialists of the November days and proselytes of every description: you can see that the acquisition of a new judgment of values may be the affair of an hour! And for that reason one must not criticize them too closely—unless they try to make a profit out of their conversion.

All social judgments presuppose a system of recognized values. The values of Christian ethics have never penetrated deeply into the collective judgment of mankind; even in the mediæval bloom of Christian, or rather of ecclesiastical, culture the moral conceptions of Christianity remained the possession of a few chosen spirits and communities; society in general accepted the mythical element, did homage to the hierarchy, and remained ethically pagan, the upper classes being guided by a code of honour resting on the worship of courage. The Churches never made any serious effort to shape an ethical code; they were preoccupied with the teaching of dogmas of faith which carried them ever farther and farther from the groundwork of the Gospels, and they devoted whatever surplus energies they had to politics, and to accommodations with the ruling powers of the world.

The cult of courage imposed on and exercised by the ruling classes, and symbolically imaged in their code of honour, took an effective shape in the banning of cowardice and of cowardly crime. So far as positive values go, the ethics of nobility degenerated into smartness, the claim for "satisfaction" and the exclusiveness of rank; a Prussian and Kantian abstraction, the conception of duty, a conception at bottom unproved and incapable of generating conviction, became a rule of life, made effective by training and control. The ruling powers and their controls have given way, and their dry brittleness is revealed.

We have not succeeded in finding a substitute for social ethics in an idealized type of national character. The imagination of the Western nations, like those of antiquity, has shaped ideal types which they believe or would wish themselves to resemble; they know what they mean by "esprit gaulois," or "English character," or "American Democracy," while, in accordance with the problematic character of our being, we Germans, except for the statuesque heroes of legendary times, or certain historic but inimitable figures, have conceived or poetically created no character of which we can say that it embodies the collective spirit of Germany.

The super-ethical doctrine of the being, the growth and the empire of the soul has been laid down by us, but there are as yet few into whose consciousness it has penetrated; the transformation of thought and feeling which must proceed from it will not lay hold of the masses directly, but will filter continually from one social stratum to another.

The recognized values of social judgment! It sounds so abstract, so remote from practice, that one might well believe we were landed again in the cloudland of festal oratory and the emotions of the leading article. The voluntary recognition of an invisible authority! And this after we have shattered the visible, and are living in the midst of intellectual anarchy and moral Nihilism! And yet moral valuations, simple, binding, and on the level of social judgment, are near enough to be within our grasp.

Are not all the four quarters of the world to-day talking about Democracy? Have not we ourselves got tired of this word, forbidden till a year ago—tired, even in circles where the modest word "Liberal" was never pronounced without a frown? And what does Democracy mean? Do we take it in the merely negative sense, that one is no longer obliged to put up with things? Or in the meagre sense, that responsibility goes by favour, and that the majority must decide? Or the dubious sense, that we are yearning to make our way through a sham Socialism to the Dollar Republic?

It is not the form of government, it is the form of society, that determines the spirit of a land. There is no democratic form of society, for democracy can be in league with capitalism, with socialism, or even with the class of clubs and castes. The unspoken fundamental conception which gives significance and stability both to the forms of a democratic constitution and to those of an organic society is called Solidarity—that is to say, cohesion and the sense of community. Solidarity means that each man does not come first in his own eyes, but before God and State and himself each man must stand and be answerable for all, and all for each.

In this sense of solidarity the dominion of the majority over the minority is not an object to be striven for but an evil to be avoided; the true object of a solid democracy is the dominion of a people over itself, not by reckoning up the relative strength of its various interests, but by virtue of the spirit and of the will which it sets free. In this sense of solidarity no society can be based on hereditary monopolies either of capital or of cultivation; nor can it be delivered over to the terrorism of vocations and unions which, under the leaderships of shouters, claim the right whenever they please, to strangle indispensable industries; nor can it be based on demagogic flattery of excitable mobs. Every born man must from his cradle onwards have the same right to existence; he must be sheltered and fostered as he grows up, and be free to choose his lot. Every occupation must be open to him, except that he must not encroach on the sphere of another man's liberty. The standard of his activity is not to be fixed by birth or privilege or force or cunning or the glib tongue, but again, by spirit and by will.

To-day, while cultivation of the spirit is still a class-monopoly, it cannot form any standard of creative capacity. And yet it has been demonstrated that so powerful is the passion for culture in a spirit which is in any degree qualified for it, that even to-day it is capable, by self-education, of surmounting some of the artificial barriers. There was not, to my knowledge, any illiterate among the Prussian or German Ministers of the new era, and the one of them who excused his deficiencies of language with the class-monopoly of education was in the wrong, for any man of normal capacity might in ten years' practice of popular oratory have learned the elements of syntax.

When access to the cultivation of the German spirit has become a common right of the whole people, Culture will become, if not the sign at least the presupposition of creative activity. The proof of capacity will then cease to be settled either between agitators and the masses, or in the dimness of privileged chanceries, but in the productive competition of men of high intellectual endowment.

Society will not be divided by classes and castes, it will not be graded according to pedigree or possessions, it will not be ruled by separate interests; by ideas or by the masses; it will be an ordered body—ordered by spirit, by will, by service and responsibility.

Any one who does not accept this self-created and self-renewing order, and who at the same time rejects the old, is simply working for the dominion of force and chance. A society can no more remain permanently without order than the staff of a factory or the crew of a ship. Only instead of an organic order we may have an accidental and arbitrary, an order of the personal type, springing from the dexterity shown in some favourable moment, maintaining itself by force, and seeking to perpetuate itself in some form of hereditary oligarchy.

An order of the priestly and hierarchical type is no longer thinkable to-day, nor can one of the peasant type come into question in a land of urban industry. Whoever wishes to see an organic self-determining and self-regenerating order of society, has therefore to choose between the military order, resting upon disciplined bodily capacity, or the mercantile and capitalist order which rests upon business-sense and egoistic alertness, or the demagogic order which rests upon the rhetorical domination of the masses, and does not last long as it soon turns to violence and oligarchy, or finally the order of culture, resting upon spirit, character, and education.

This last is not merely the only suitable one for us and the only one which is worthy of our past; it will also in time become the general order of society prevailing over all the world. In the vision of this order we recognize the mission that Prussia neglected, though it lay within its grasp for a hundred years; what it neglected and the rock on which it foundered.

The greatness of Prussian policy since 1713 lay in its premonition and appreciation of the principle of mechanism even before it became common to all the world. Organization and improvement, the war machine and money, science, practicality and conscientiousness—all this is clearly mechanization seen from the political side.

The early application of these principles was a stroke of genius far in advance of the then condition of the world. Seen from this standpoint, all the rest of the continental world, not yet mechanized, and burdened with the relics of mediævalism, Cæsarism and clericalism, seemed torpid and lost in illusions: arbitrary, inaccurate and slovenly. With short interruptions this Prusso-central point of view was maintained until the middle of the World-War; and not quite unjustly, for Prussia remained in every respect ahead of other powers in the department of mechanization.

For a hundred years the Prussian principles had a monopoly of success; elsewhere they were scarcely understood and much less imitated. Then came Napoleon.

He took over the mechanistic principle and handled it as never a man had done before; he became the mechanizer of the world. At the same time he was something mightier than that: he was the heir of the French idea of spiritual and popular liberty.

Prussia fell, and would have fallen, even if its mechanism had not grown rusty. Its leaders learnt their lessons from France and England, they set on foot a liberation of the people by departmental authority and a liberation of the spirit by the people; they put new life into the mechanism, and they conquered with the help of England as we have lately seen France conquer with the help of America.

But here came a parting of the ways. It was possible to pursue either the way of mechanization or that of the liberation of the spirit. Prussia did neither; it stood still. In the place of the liberation of the spirit came the reaction; in the place of mechanization came the bureaucracy. On the rest of the Continent, too, the movement for political mechanization was stifled, the force that stifled it being the uprising economic movement.

Bismarck was aware of the untried forces that lay in the system of political mechanization. The world, as we looked at it from our Prussian window, seemed as loose and slovenly as ever, and it was so. Once again, with a mighty effort, the Prussian mechanism was revived and the movement of the bourgeoisie towards liberty and the life of the spirit was repressed. This was called "realism" in politics, and the estimate was a just one. There was no progress to be made with professional Liberalism; but with Krupp and Roon one organized victories. As in Frederick's time the slovenly Continent had to give way, Prussia mounted to the climax of her fortunes, and won Germany.

And again there was a parting of the ways; but this time there was no one to stand for civic and spiritual freedom. People believed they had all they wanted of it; democracy was discredited and broken, the professors were political realists, success followed the side of mechanization, which was rightly supposed to be linked with the dynasty, and mechanization in the economic sphere drew to its side the hope of gain.

Bismarck died in the midst of anxieties, but to the end he had no scruples. The two systems of mechanization were at their zenith, and the other countries looked, in political affairs, as slovenly as ever. One was wearing itself out in parliamentary conflicts, another had no battle-cruisers, another was lacking in cannon, or in recruits, or in railways, or in finances; the trains never came in up to time, everywhere one found public opinion or the Press interfering in process of law or in the administration, everywhere there were scandals; in Prussian Germany alone was everything up to the mark.

Only one thing was overlooked. The mechanization of economics had become a common possession for everybody. Starting from this and with the methods and experiences attached to it, it was possible also for other countries, if necessary, to mechanize their politics or, as we say now, to militarize them. And this could be done with even more life and vigour than in Prussia, whose organization was there believed to be inimitable and where the principle of mechanism was, as it were, stored up in tins and in some places was obviously getting mouldy. In the matter of Freedom, however, the other peoples were ahead of us, and to the political isolation of Prussia spiritual isolation was now added.

In the encircling fog which prevailed on economic developments there was not a single statesman who recognized that Prussian principles had ceased to be a monopoly, or an advantage, not to mention a conception of genius. This lack of perception was the political cause of the war. Instead of renewing ourselves inwardly through freedom and the spirit, and carrying on a defensive policy as quietly, discreetly, and inconspicuously as possible, we took to arming and hurrahing. Worse than any playing of false notes was the mistake we made in key and in tempo: D major, *Allegro, Marcia, Fortissimo*, with cymbals and trumpets!

To-day we have no longer a choice before us, only a decision. The period of mechanical Prussianization is over for us, the period of the mechanical policy of Force is over for all the world, although the heliographs of Versailles seem to reflect it high above the horizon. It is not a capitalistic Peace of God as imagined by the international police which has now begun; it is the social epoch. In this epoch the people will live and will range themselves according to the strength of the ideas which they stand for.

It is not enough for us to become Germans instead of Prussians; not even if, as it were to be desired, we should succeed in rescuing from the collapse of Prussia her genuine virtues of practicality, order and duty. It is not enough to brew some soulless mixture out of the worn-out methods of the Western bourgeoisie and the unripe attempts of Eastern revolutionaries. It is not enough—no, it will lead us to destruction quicker than any one believes—to blunder along with the disgusting bickerings of interests and the complacent narrowness of officialism, talking one day of the rate of exchange, another of our debts, and the next of the food question, plugging one hole with the stopping of another and lying down at night with a sigh of relief: Well, something's got done; all will come right.

No, unthinking creatures that you are; nothing will come right until you drop your insincere chatter, your haggling, your agitating and compromising, and begin to think. Here is a people that has lost the basis of its existence, because, in its blind faith in authority, it staked that existence on prosperity and power; and both are gone. Do you want to stake *our* existence, on ships, soldiers, mines, trade-connexions, which we no longer possess, or upon the soil, of which we have not enough, or upon our broken will to work? Are we to be the labour-serfs and the serfage stud-farm of the world? Only on Thoughts and Ideals can our existence be staked. Where is your thought? Where is the thought of Germany?

We can and must live only by becoming what we were designed to be, what we were about to be, what we failed to become: a people of the Spirit, the Spirit among the peoples of mankind. That is the thought of Germany.

This thought is shaping the New Society—the society of the spirit and the cultivation of the spirit, the only one which can hold its ground in the new epoch, and which fulfils it.

This is why we have been endowed with a character whose will is weak in external things and strong in inward responsibility; why depth and understanding, practicality and uprightness, many-sidedness and individuality, power of work and invention, imagination and aspiration have been bestowed upon us, in order that we may fulfil these things. For what do these qualities, as a whole, betoken? Not the conqueror, not the statesman, not the worldling, and not the man of business; it is a narrow and trivial misuse of all faculty for us to pretend to represent these types among the nations. They betoken the labourers of the spirit; and far as we are from being a nation of thinkers and poets, it is nevertheless our right and our high calling to be a thinking nation among the nations.

But on what, you may ask with scorn, is this thinking nation to live? With all its wisdom, will it not be reduced to beggary and starvation?

No—it will live. That people which amid a century of world-revolution is able to form for itself a stable, well-balanced, ordered and highly developed form of society will be one that works and produces. All around there will be quarrelling and conflict, there will be little work and little production. For the next decade the question will be, not where is the demand but where is the supply?

The countries are laid waste, as Germany was after the Thirty Years' War; only we do not as yet recognize it, so long as the fever lasts we do not notice the decline.

Production, thought-out and penetrated with spirit, on the part of a highly developed society, and combined with labour-fellowship, is more than valuable production or cheap production; it is something exemplary and essential. And this applies not only to production itself but to the methods of production, to the technique, the schooling, the organization, the manner of thinking.

It is a petty thing to say that we were destroyed out of envy. Why did not envy destroy America and England? The world regarded us at once with admiration and with repulsion; with admiration for our systematic and laborious ways, with repulsion for our tradesman-like obtrusiveness, the brusque and dangerous character of our leadership and the ostentatious servility with which we endured it. If it had been possible anywhere outside of our naked, mercantile and national egoism to discover a German idea, it would have been respected.

The German idea of cultivation of the spirit will win something for us which we have not known for a century, and the scope of which we cannot yet measure; people will freely appreciate us, they will further us and follow us on our way. We have no idea what it means for a people to have these sympathetic forces at its side, as France had in its creation of forms, England and America in civilization and democracy, Russia in Slavonic orthodoxy and the neutral States in their internationalism.

There is no fear: we shall live, and more than live. For the first time for centuries we shall again be conscious of a mission, and around all our internal oppositions will be twined a bond which will be something more than a bond of interest.

The goal of the world-revolution upon which we have now entered means in its material aspect the melting of all strata of society into one. In its transcendental aspect it means redemption: redemption of the lower strata to freedom and to the spirit. No one can redeem himself but every one can redeem another. Class for class, man for man: thus is a people redeemed. Yet in each case there must be readiness and in each there must be good-will.

FOOTNOTES:

1918, when the revolution in Germany broke out at Kiel.

THE END

THE EUROPEAN LIBRARY

Edited by J. E. SPINGARN

This series is intended to introduce foreign authors whose works are not accessible in English, and in general to keep Americans in touch with the intellectual and spiritual ferment of the continent of Europe. No attempt will be made to give what Americans miscall "the best books," if by this is meant conformity to some high and illusory standard of past greatness; any twentieth-century book which displays creative power or a new outlook or more than ordinary interest or charm will be eligible for inclusion. Nor will the attempt be made to select books that merely confirm American standards of taste or morals, since the series is intended to serve as a mirror of European culture and not as a glass through which it may be seen darkly. Fiction will predominate, but belles lettres, poetry, philosophy, social and economic discussion, history, biography, and other fields will be represented.

"The first organized effort to bring into English a series of the really significant figures in contemporary European literature.... An undertaking as creditable and as ambitious as any of its kind on the other side of the Atlantic."—New York Evening Post.

THE WORLD'S ILLUSION. By J. WASSERMANN. Translated by Ludwig Lewisohn. Two volumes. (Second printing.)

One of the most remarkable creative works of our time, revolving about the experiences of a man who sums up the wealth and culture of our age yet finds them wanting. The first volume depicts the life of the upper classes of European society, the second is a very Inferno of the Slums; and the whole mirrors, with extraordinary insight, the beauty and sorrow, the power and weakness of our social and spiritual world. "A human comedy in the great sense, which no modern can afford not to hear."—H. W. Boynton, in the Weekly Review.

PEOPLE. By PIERRE HAMP. Translated by James Whitall. With an Introduction by Elizabeth Shepley Sergeant.

Introducing one of the most significant writers of France, himself a working man, who in these stories of the French underworld expresses the new self-consciousness of the worker's outlook.

THE NEW SOCIETY. By WALTER RATHENAU. Translated by Arthur Windham.

One of Germany's most influential thinkers and men of action presents his vision of the new society emerging out of the War.

DECADENCE AND OTHER ESSAYS ON THE CULTURE OF IDEAS. By REMY DE GOURMONT. Translated by William Aspenwall Bradley.

The first authorized version of the critical work of one of the great aesthetic thinkers of France.

IN PREPARATION

THE PATRIOT. By HEINRICH MANN. Translated by Ernest A. Boyd.

The career of a typical product of militarism, in school, university, business, patriotism, and love, told with a biting incisiveness and irony.

THE REFORM OF EDUCATION. By GIOVANNI GENTILE. With an Introduction by BENEDETTO CROCE. Translated by Dino Bigongiari.

A new interpretation of the meaning of education, by one who shares with Croce the leadership of Italian thought to-day.

A POET'S LOVES: FROM THE UNPUBLISHED MANUSCRIPTS OF VICTOR HUGO. By LOUIS BARTHOU. Translated by Daniel Créhange Rosenthal.

A striking, not to say sensational, revelation of the intimate private life of a great poet, by an ex-Premier of France.

Lightning Source UK Ltd.
Milton Keynes UK
UKHW010746271222
414464UK00004B/270